BALAAM'S GOD

PROPHETIC INSIGHTS FROM AN INFAMOUS LIFE

JONATHAN AMMON

LOWERLIGHT BOOKS

For Tatiana

CONTENTS

Acknowledgments	vii
Introducing Balaam	ix
1. The Story Begins	1
2. Who Was Balaam?	21
3. Defining Divination	37
4. Balaam Meets Yahweh	59
5. Balaam's Donkey	75
6. Balaam's First Oracle	89
7. Balaam's Second Oracle	105
8. Balaam's Third Oracle	117
9. Balaam's Final Words	131
10. Balaam's Final Actions	139
11. Balaam's End	155
12. Balaam's Way	169
Epilogue: The True Prophet of God	187
Appendix: Balaam's Fourth Oracle: An Exegetical Analysis of Numbers 24:12-19	199
Selected Bibliography	221
From the Author	225
About the Author	227

Balaam's God: Prophetic Insights from an Infamous Life by Jonathan Ammon

Published by Lowerlight Books

© 2019 Jonathan Ammon

All rights reserved. No portion of this book may be reproduced in any form without permission from the publisher, except as permitted by U.S. copyright law. For permissions contact:

JonathanandTatianaAmmon@gmail.com

Paperback ISBN: 9781694654267

Cover Design by Jacob Thomas

All Scripture quotations unless otherwise noted are taken from The Holy Bible, English Standard Version® (ESV®)

Copyright © 2001 by Crossway, a publishing ministry of Good News Publishers.

All rights reserved.

ESV Text Edition: 2016

The Holy Bible, English Standard Version (ESV) is adapted from the Revised Standard Version of the Bible, copyright Division of Christian Education of the National Council of the Churches of Christ in the U.S.A. All rights reserved.

Scripture quotations marked (NKJV) are taken from the New King James Version. Copyright © 1982 by Thomas Nelson, Inc. Used by permission. All rights reserved.

ACKNOWLEDGMENTS

I am tremendously thankful to my wife Tatiana who has learned to be patient with a husband whose mind is often somewhere else. I also want to acknowledge my church and all the members who were beta readers, as well as my family and extended friends and readers who carefully read and critiqued the manuscript. Thanks to Art Thomas for his generosity and never flagging faith in me, and for his hard work and support in writing. Many thanks go to Jesus. May You be glorified.

INTRODUCING BALAAM

Balaam built his spell step by step. He kept a fire of sacred wood burning. The shadow of his hand crept across a knife and an ordered pile of animal organs. The warmth of the fire had baked blood into his fingerprints. The animal sacrifices were over. Night was coming quickly. He was alone. But he wouldn't be for long.

He knelt before the fire and began his ritual. Balaam pursued the gods in the haunted dark.

The next morning the crowd found him awake, his face stained with tears.

"Sit down," he told them, "I will tell you what the gods are about to do. Come and see the wonders of the gods..."

INTRODUCING BALAAM

In fasting and grief Balaam foretold drought and darkness overtaking the land. He spoke of mourning and death. The whole of nature would be turned upside down. Disaster would reign. All sense of order would be lost.

But Balaam did more than foretell. His spells went further than just prediction. He worked his magic to change the future, to combat the will of the gods. He implored the goddesses Ashtar of Moab and Sheger to bless in the place of cursing...

The Transcription of Deir Alla stops there. The above is my fictionalized interpretation of its contents.[1] While difficult to read and harder to interpret, it stands as a testament to Balaam's fame or infamy.[2] Along with pagan texts like *The Transcription of Deir Alla*, Balaam is mentioned in the *Talmud* and throughout Jewish commentary and history. His name appears in the *Quran*.[3] In the Bible, his name appears a surprising number of times outside of the narrative of Numbers 22-25 where his story connects most with the story of Israel.[4]

The Transcription of Deir Alla is not Scripture and cannot be treated as a sound source, but it does reveal that Balaam was perceived as a powerful communicator with the gods. The story also shows Balaam in more of a prophetic or oracular role than a simple diviner or sorcerer. He was thought to be able to encounter the gods at night, see the future, and report it. More than that, he was believed to be able to impact the gods and the outcome of their behavior.

A number of historical documents speak of Balaam, but they each present Balaam from a certain spiritual lens and interpretation. For believers, the Bible is our only sure source of accurate information about Balaam. But *The Transcription of Deir Alla* is surprisingly consistent with a historical reading of the biblical text. Balaam does have a reputation for being able to bless and curse with the power of the gods. And in Numbers, he does seek Yahweh at night, and arrived in the morning with prophetic words from the one true God.

There is a reason Balaam remains so infamous. The issues of his heart are the issues that God's servants face today. The Bible uses Balaam's name and story to teach about true and false ministry, referencing a history that reveals the complexity of life.

Balaam is not a simple villain. While the New Testament exclusively mentions him as a negative example—a false minister—there is a lot to admire in Balaam's story. Balaam may be the most infamous false teacher in biblical history, yet he was not condemned for his ignorance or powerlessness. His story reveals that the fact he got so many things right ultimately brought him under greater condemnation. To whom much is given, much shall be required (Luke 12:48).

Despite his pursuit of other gods, many contemporary prophetic ministers may not come as close to faithful ministry as Balaam did.

This book will examine Balaam's life for the good and the bad —where Balaam came from, what he got right, what he got wrong, and how his story applies to our lives and ministries today. This book looks closely at the life of a man who heard from God and delivered national prophetic words that became Scripture. And the life of a man who became a false teacher and a false prophet. It's about faithfulness in prophetic ministry.

The Bible remains the only fully reliable source for training about prophetic ministry and the only fully reliable source for information about Balaam. This book will examine Balaam's life from his first appearance in Numbers 22 through the final mentions of his name in Jude and Revelation. We will travel through Balaam's story passage by passage and verse by verse, pulling out the themes and lessons applicable to prophetic ministry today. Though we will move forward through Balaam's story in Numbers, I will often pull in passages from the New Testament or other Old Testament books to help interpret and illuminate different parts of Balaam's story and how they relate to God's prophetic people in the New Covenant. This book follows Balaam's story as told by God's Word, expounding on the message God has for His people from Balaam's life.

INTRODUCING BALAAM

Balaam's God is a story. Balaam's life is too complex for simple moral lessons, and its sections don't fit into easy topical chapters. Like Hebrew literature, this book will identify a theme as it arises in the text, move on with the action of the story, and then revisit that theme as it arises—again and again. The story will pause from time to time to give clear biblical teaching about a necessary topic, but the story itself will set our course. This book will draw out the main points of the narrative but will not address some difficult issues that arise from the text, like violence and judgment in the Old Testament. I hold nuanced views on these subjects but present the violence in a straightforward reading rather than wrestling with different interpretations and understandings of Old Testament violence.

While I hope this book will be accessible to everyone, it does not focus on the basics of hearing God's voice or prophetic ministry. There are powerful and practical lessons about hearing God's voice in Balaam's story and in this book. But if you primarily want a basic and practical book on the prophetic, I have to point you to a book I contributed to with Art Thomas and James Loruss, *Voice of God,* and my previous book on the prophetic and holiness, *Prophetic Transformation.* This book is more advanced teaching about the character of prophetic ministry.

This text has a strong academic foundation, but it is not an academic book. It's meant for everyone who seeks to serve the Lord faithfully. There is a wealth of academic studies about

INTRODUCING BALAAM

Balaam. As I pursued research for this book, I had to make a decision. What scholarship was the most valuable? How could I sort through the differing conclusions and perspectives on the prophet?

The most effective way to narrow down the research was with the simple conviction that *every single thing the Bible says about Balaam is true and accurate*. This book approaches the different passages about Balaam in the Bible as coherent and harmonious. That narrowed down the research quite a bit, and you can find a bibliography at the back of this book. If I were to recommend a single resource that was most useful to me and to this book it would be Ronald Allen's commentary on the book of Numbers and his dissertation on Balaam's Oracles.

This book uses research as its foundation, but this book's purpose is practical. I want to present the story of Balaam in a fresh way that pulls revelation from his life about prophets, prophetic ministry, and persevering in faithfulness to the true God, Jesus Christ (1 John 5:20).

We will take a careful look at who Balaam was before and after the story in Numbers 22-24, but first we must look at the story of God's people. As Israel travels to and then around the border of the Promised Land, Balaam sits in darkness at the edge of their story, ready to enter at a key point and cast a shadow that looms across history.

---

1. Cole, Dennis R. Numbers: An Exegetical and Theological Exposition of Holy Scripture: 3 (The New American Commentary) (Kindle Location 10491). B&H Publishing Group. Kindle Edition.
2. Allen, Ronald B. (The Expositor's Bible Commentary) (Kindle Locations 9812-9817). Zondervan. Kindle Edition.
3. Allen, Ronald Barclay. The Theology of the Balaam Oracles: A Pagan Diviner and the Word of God (Unpublished doctoral dissertation) p. 3. Dallas Theological Seminary, Dallas.
4. Numbers 31:8 and 16, Deuteronomy 23:4-5, Joshua 13:22, Joshua 24:9-10, Nehemiah 13:2, Micah 6:5, 2 Peter 2:15, Jude 1:11, Revelation 2:14

ONE

THE STORY BEGINS

In the Wilderness

The Hebrew title of the Book of Numbers translates to *In the Wilderness*.[1] God made a promise to the unbelieving and rebellious Israelites, "...your dead bodies shall fall in this wilderness. And your children shall be shepherds in the wilderness forty years and shall suffer for your faithlessness, until the last of your dead bodies lies in the wilderness" (Numbers 14:32-33). The Book of Numbers describes this journey to the Promised Land, the loss of the Promised Land, and the forty years of life, death and judgment in the wilderness.

Numbers can be divided into five sections. Three sections contain the stories of Israel's life and God's law-giving in the wilderness. Two sections tell of Israel's journeys between these times in the wilderness. Israel's journey from Sinai to Kadesh, where the Promised Land was lost, and the second journey from Kadesh to the Plains of Moab. On the Plains of Moab, Israel's journey comes to a climax in an encounter with Balaam and finishes with the next generation waiting to enter the Promised Land under Joshua's leadership.

- Section 1: Law-giving at Sinai (Exodus 19:1-Numbers 10:10)
- Section 2: Journey from Sinai to Kadesh (Numbers 10:11-12:16)
- Section 3: Law-giving at Kadesh (Numbers 13:1-19:22)
- Section 4: Journey from Kadesh to the Plains of Moab (Numbers 20:1-22:1)
- Section 5: Law-giving on the Plains of Moab (Numbers 22:2-36:13)

Sinai to Kadesh

After God led Israel out of Egypt they formed a covenant with Him at Mount Sinai, received the Ten Commandments, and built the tabernacle in the wilderness. They spent a year at Sinai, and in preparation for moving into the Promised Land, they "numbered the people" or took a census. The Book of Numbers gets its Greek name and our English derivation from this census. [2]

This section also includes detailed instructions for how Israel was to organize their camp, and their travel as they started the journey. The tabernacle and God's presence resided at the center of the camp, the priests and Levites surrounded it, and the rest of the tribes encircled the outer circle of the camp. The cloud of God's presence hovered above the tabernacle and then moved out from the center with the Israelites following. The cloud of God's presence was led by the Ark of the Covenant and the Levites.

God's presence led Israel, and they centered themselves in His presence at every stop. God laid out meticulous organization to keep Israel living and moving in His presence. God has a similar plan to order our lives around our experience with Him.

The Israelites started their journey from Sinai to Kadesh in the wilderness of Paran. In fewer than three days the Israelites began to complain about "their misfortunes." God sent fire to consume the outer edges of their camp. The fire crept inward until Moses interceded for the people. The fire halted and went out. They named the place Taberah or "burning," so they would remember God's judgment, but His people quickly forgot.

"Now the rabble that was among them had a strong craving. And the people of Israel also wept again and said, 'Oh that we had meat to eat!'" (Numbers 11:4). Their complaints went on in detail. They demanded better food than the miraculously provided manna. What happened next foreshadowed the promise of a prophetic people in the New Covenant and the purpose of this book.

You May All Prophesy

Part of the solution to Israel's constant complaints and Moses' prophetic burden for the people involved gathering the seventy elders that Moses had appointed to help him lead.[3] These elders gathered around the tabernacle in expectation. In an experience that none of them had known before, God placed His Spirit upon all seventy. Overflowing with the Spirit of God, they began to prophesy without premeditation or experience. It must have been holy chaos.

Seventy men who had never experienced the Holy Spirit upon them suddenly received the words of God. Moses' protégé, Joshua, was upset and told Moses to stop them. Joshua thought that only Moses, the prophet and leader, could prophesy. Moses reflected the heart of God when he replied, "Oh, that all the Lord's people were prophets and that the Lord would put his Spirit upon them!" (Numbers 11:29). Moses expressed the desire and plan of God to be accomplished centuries later in a New Covenant.

When God poured out His Spirit on the day of Pentecost, He fulfilled the words of the prophet Joel: "I will pour out my Spirit on all flesh, and your sons and your daughters shall prophesy" (Acts 2:16-17 NKJV). The empowerment of the Spirit was poured out and made available to all.

We all were given access to the Spirit and His gifts. To qualify for spiritual gifts—and specifically for prophecy—we need only to be "sons and daughters" and receive the gift that God has poured out. When God's Spirit rests upon you, this is as simple as believing the truth that you can prophesy. You can listen to what God is saying and tell someone else for their encouragement. That is prophecy (1 Corinthians 14:3).

When God's Spirit comes upon us, we can be used by God to speak His word. God can use each of us to speak the truth for His glory. In Kadesh God used seventy elders. In Moab he used a pagan diviner to prophesy. On the road to Moab a donkey proclaimed what she saw in the spiritual world.

Stopped at Canaan

The joy of prophecy overflowing from newly appointed and anointed leaders was amplified by a strong wind from God that overwhelmed the camp with quail. It took the people two days and a night to gather all the quail. The least anyone gathered was 60 bushels or 480 dry gallons of quail.[4]

They set up a feast.

As they were chewing the meat, death spread around the camp. God had sent a plague that interrupted their feast. The timing of God's judgment made His thoughts known.

The Israelites named the place "Graves of Craving." Not all prosperity lasts, and not all prosperity is blessing. God used their desire for pleasure to judge them.

This same desire brought judgment on Balaam of Peor. This same desire brings discipline on God's people today. If we do not receive that discipline, it will bring judgment on us on the last day.

Mouth to Mouth

God's new gift of prophetically anointed elders promised new leadership, but also provoked jealousy. Moses was no longer the only person to hear God's voice. Others prophesied as well as Moses. What made his relationship with God better than theirs?

Pride and jealousy crept into Miriam and Aaron's hearts, and they began to question Moses' authority. They knew Moses better than the others. He was more human to them. Miriam was Moses's sister and had been part of rescuing and raising him. Aaron knew his brother-in-law's struggles, and they both found an opportunity to be offended with Moses because of his "Cushite wife" (this was probably a second wife, perhaps taken after his first wife's death).[5]

Miriam and Aaron were confident in their prophetic gifting, and they were surrounded by a greater prophetic community. "Has the LORD indeed spoken only through Moses? Has he not spoken through us also?" (Numbers 12:2). They were right. God had not only spoken through Moses. God had spoken through them. They misinterpreted these facts to mean that God spoke to all of them equally or that God had given them all equal authority.

Many of us make the same mistake today. We value democracy and equality so much that we fail to realize that God has sovereignly gifted some above others and that God has sovereignly called some to greater positions of leadership than others. "In humility value others above yourselves" (Phil 2:3b).

God chose Moses for a unique role and calling. He called and anointed others around Moses to support him, not to usurp him. God's response to their rebellion revealed this and much more.

> And the LORD heard it (Numbers 11:2).

God called Moses, Miriam, and Aaron at the same time, instructing them to come to the Tent of Meeting. He came down in a pillar of cloud, and called Aaron and Miriam to come close before giving a striking endorsement of Moses and his ministry:

> And He said, "Hear my words: If there is a prophet among you, I the Lord make myself known to him in a vision; I speak with him in a dream. Not so with my servant Moses. He is faithful in all my house. With him I speak mouth to mouth,

clearly, and not in riddles, and he beholds the form of the Lord. Why then were you not afraid to speak against my servant Moses?" (Numbers 12:6-8).

God revealed much about prophetic ministry, but even more about His relationship with Moses. God often spoke to the prophets at that time through visions and dreams. This kind of revelation often contained symbols and needed interpretation. His communication with Moses was clear and direct. It did not need interpretation, and many believe that this indicates Moses and God had verbal conversations in which God spoke audibly to Moses for extended periods of time. At the very least, God and Moses had an intimate relationship that couldn't be compared to other prophets. Miriam and Aaron knew this, and the appropriate response should have been respect.

God has poured out His Spirit and His Spirit's gifts out on His people. We should rejoice in these gifts. We should receive these gifts with faith and joy. But we should also be careful to receive these gifts with humility.

When God's gifts become common, some lose respect for their leader's calling and authority. They think, "My relationship with God is as good or better than his or hers. I hear God as much as he or she does." They lose respect for God's gifting in general. They prophesy, and they find less respect for others who do so as well. They fail to acknowledge that others are gifted and called in different ways than they are. They fail to see that God has given more responsibility to some than others. They have no reverence for God's calling.

Miriam and Aaron had acted against Moses. They spoke. And God heard them. God also hears how we speak about our own leaders. Miriam and Aaron wanted their leadership to change —not because of God's will for His people but because of their own selfish and proud desires. They intended to usurp God's appointed leadership, and God disciplined them.

When God finished speaking, Miriam had leprosy. Moses begged for God to spare her, and God did. Miriam had to spend seven days outside the camp awaiting purification, and the nation sat and waited for her, reminded of their rebellion.

Spies Sent into Canaan

Ronald Allen prefaces his commentary on Numbers Chapter 13 with a reminder of what a zenith this was in Israel's history and in God's faithfulness:

> We appear to be at a new beginning of greatness for Israel when we enter this chapter. The vindication of Moses as the servant of Yahweh had been stunning and unforgettable. The presence of the people in the vastness of their numbers there on the plateau of Paran was undeniable. The desire of the people to enter the Land of Promise was unquestionable. The faithfulness of the Lord to his promise and his commitment to his people were sure and unalterable. Given

all the experiences the people had gone through in the previous months of preparation and journey, at last— at long last— it was time for them to claim Yahweh's word, to believe in his power, to march in his name, and to enter his land.⁶

This was the moment they had been waiting for. They no longer had to ask, "Are we there yet?" They were at the edge of the entering the promise.

> The Lord spoke to Moses, saying, "Send men to spy out the land of Canaan, which I am giving to the people of Israel. From each tribe of their fathers you shall send a man, every one a chief among them." So Moses sent them from the wilderness of Paran, according to the command of the Lord, all of them men who were heads of the people of Israel (Numbers 13:1-3).

Deuteronomy records a speech that Moses gave many years later Moses reflecting on Israel's arrival at Canaan with a more detailed summary of what happened. While Numbers clearly and succinctly states that "The Lord spoke to Moses saying..." the account in Deuteronomy goes a little differently, highlighting God's gracious partnership with us in hearing His voice.

> "Then we set out from Horeb and went through all that great and terrifying wilderness that you saw, on the way to the hill country of the Amorites, as the Lord our God commanded

> us. And we came to Kadesh-barnea. And I said to you, 'You have come to the hill country of the Amorites, which the Lord our God is giving us. See, the Lord your God has set the land before you. Go up, take possession, as the Lord, the God of your fathers, has told you. Do not fear or be dismayed.'" (Deuteronomy 1:19-20).

The first command that Moses gave was not that they send agents to report on the Promised Land, but that they go out and take it. This was the land that God had promised them. He had told them about its goodness, and about His desire to bless Israel with this land as home. They didn't need to investigate. They could act on His word and take the land immediately. How history would have been different if they had boldly acted on what they knew of God's will.

> Then all of you came near me and said, 'Let us send men before us, that they may explore the land for us and bring us word again of the way by which we must go up and the cities into which we shall come.' The thing seemed good to me, and I took twelve men from you, one man from each tribe (Deuteronomy 1:19-23).

Instead of obeying Moses' orders, the people came to Moses and asked to send agents into Canaan to discover the best way to approach the land to take it. Moses felt that this was wise and chose leaders from among the people to enter Canaan first.

But in Numbers the command to send the men into the land was clearly made by Yahweh. Does the Bible contradict itself here?

The Bible presents the same story from two different perspectives. Numbers presents the story from the divine perspective. God spoke, and it was done.[7]

Deuteronomy presents the story from the people of Israel's perspective. The people made a request to send men to explore the land. Moses decided this request was a valid one and took it into his intimate relationship with God.

When we consider both accounts together we see that the agents of the people were part of God's grace. He answers our petitions. He works with us, using us to accomplish His will.

The Bible is full of these kinds of stories, and full of God's grace as He gives us freedom to pursue His will. We must take caution though. Some of what God allows is ultimately not for our best. Some of what God says "yes" to, trades God's best plan for human comfort. Moses' request to speak through Aaron, Israel's request for a king, and Balaam's story should caution us to use discernment to find and pursue God's best plan with immediate obedience and full conviction.

The Spies Report

> Then the Lord said to Abram, "Know for certain that your offspring will be sojourners in a land that is not theirs and

will be servants there, and they will be afflicted for four hundred years. But I will bring judgment on the nation that they serve, and afterward they shall come out with great possessions. As for you, you shall go to your fathers in peace; you shall be buried in a good old age. And they shall come back here in the fourth generation, for the iniquity of the Amorites is not yet complete" (Genesis 15:13-15).

God promised Abram in clear terms that 400 years later his descendants would come out of slavery in riches and that they would return to the land in the fourth generation. He kept His promise. Hundreds of years later, through slavery, disobedience, idolatry, rebellion, and countless sins, God remained faithful to Abraham and His people. He brought Israel through it all. He shook nature to do it, but He kept His promise. Four hundred years later, Israel's spies came to the land God had promised and the gravesites of their patriarchs.

> So they went up and spied out the land from the wilderness of Zin to Rehob, near Lebo-hamath. They went up into the Negeb and came to Hebron. Ahiman, Sheshai, and Talmai, the descendants of Anak, were there (Numbers 13:21-22).

Hebron was the burial place of Abraham and Sarah, Isaac and Rebekah, Jacob and Leah. They were in the land where their fathers and mothers were buried. After difficult centuries of slavery and travel, they were home.

But the spies didn't mention Hebron as the burial place of the patriarchs. They didn't mention God's promise, His incredible timing, or even that they had finally come home. They were distracted by the descendants of Anak and three large men. The giants of man overcame the promises of God in their hearts and minds.

How often do we stand in the fulfillment of God's promise only to turn our face away toward future trouble? How could they forget the promise? How could we?

They should have been filled with thanksgiving for where God had brought them. If only they could have seen from a higher perspective, been pulled out of the now and reflected on all that God done through the centuries. Perhaps they wouldn't have missed God's promise and missed God's plan by a generation.

What prayers has God answered in your life? What answers to prayer are you living in today? What promises have you seen fulfilled? What were you asking God for a year ago? Five years ago? Ten years ago? What seems bigger in your life, the prayers that God has answered and the promises he's kept or the problems and threats you see in the future?

> And they told him, "We came to the land to which you sent us. It flows with milk and honey, and this is its fruit (Numbers 13:27).

Two of the agents, Caleb and Joshua were full of faith in God's promise, but the other ten were terrified of the giants in the land. All they could see was the warfare they would have to face against a strong enemy. Even though God promised to drive out the inhabitants and had led them in victory, they were unwilling to risk their lives. Their fear prevailed, and panic spread through Israel.

That night the people of Israel mourned. They longed for the slavery of Egypt. They wanted to mutiny, overthrow Moses, and find a leader who would lead them back into slavery.

Even today, the people of God can seek out leaders who will not lead them into change, blessing, or the confrontation of their fears. They can choose leaders who lead them into wandering, or into bondage. In the chapters to come, another leader does rise up from outside of Israel, and he knew how to lead the people into their old desires.

Moses, Aaron, Joshua, and Caleb confronted the crowd and their fear. They courageously faced down the mob. Swept up in a fury of fear and anger, the Israelites picked up stones to kill their leaders.

In a sudden burst of fire by night, God's glory appeared at the Tent of Meeting. God was ready to pour out just wrath on Israel and form a new nation from Moses' descendants. But Moses interceded for the people as a true prophet of God, and God forgave the people. In spite of God's forgiveness of their sin, a consequence remained for their unbelief. Only Joshua and Caleb would see the

Promised Land. The rest of this generation of Israelites would wander in the wilderness, unable to enter God's promise.

God struck the agents who misled the people with plague, and they died in the camp. God restrained his wrath from the people, but he held their leaders responsible. Those who brought a message of faithlessness and fear were punished.

The Aftermath

Sobered by their experience with God and the death of the ten spies, the people desired to repent. When the morning came they decided that they wanted to be faithful. They wanted to get ready for battle and enter the Promised Land. Moses was clear with them that they must not. God would not allow them to enter. They would lose.

But they wanted to believe that God would still give them the promise. The day before they didn't believe God would give them the victory. Now faced with the consequences of their unbelief they wanted to presume on God's kindness. They didn't want to experience any consequences for their sin.

They dressed for battle, but Moses, the Ark of the Covenant, and the glory of God did not go with them.

> Then the Amalekites and the Canaanites who lived in that hill country came down and attacked them and beat them down all the way to Hormah (Numbers 14:45).

Chastened by their defeat and facing a new future in the wilderness Israel received new laws as they prepared to finish their lives in the desert. God revealed new laws of sacrifice—a reminder of God's forgiveness and foreshadowing of God's grace in Christ.

But the people of Israel still had not changed within. Their complaining and rebelliousness doomed them to repeat the same sins again and again. Much like Miriam, Korah rebelled against Moses. He and his followers didn't understand why Moses was the leader. They believed they were as holy as Moses was. And why couldn't God's Spirit use them just the same?

God killed Korah and all who followed him. In the New Testament, the apostle Peter tied Korah and Balaam together in his warning to the church about those who would lead them astray.

The people continued to complain about food and water, provoking God's anger. But his mercy prevailed, and he miraculously provided for them and healed them.

Frustrated with the people, Moses' patience frayed, and he had his own moment of rebellion by striking a rock instead of speaking to it. The rock split and provided water for God's people. But God punished Moses. He would not be allowed to enter the Promised Land either.

After all of this complaining and rebellion Israel traveled up and down the Jordan river. It was a physical boundary to the Promised Land. God would not let them cross it.

Their hearts constantly defeated them, but after that first foolhardy attempt to enter the Promised Land without God's blessing, Israel won every military battle. Israel destroyed the kings and armies of every land they entered, including some of the giants that had frightened them at the entrance to the Promised Land.

Israel was cursed to wander the wilderness, unable to enter blessing or promise, unable to conquer their rebellion or their unfaithfulness. Yet they did not lose outward battles. God was with them in war and would not let them be destroyed. The news of their escape from Egypt spread through the land, and their victories up and down the Jordan shook the country with fear.

The news of Israel's victories and the power of their God reached the Moabites. Their king, Balak of Moab, knew he would be defeated without the help of a higher power. So he sought out the greatest spiritual figure he knew—Balaam of Peor.

---

1. Wenham, Gordon J. Numbers (Tyndale Old Testament Commentaries) (p. 15). InterVarsity Press. Kindle Edition.
2. Ibid.
3. Part of this section has been previously published in the book Voice of God.

4. Crossway Bibles. 2007. ESV: Study Bible : English standard version. Wheaton, Ill: Crossway Bibles.
5. Allen, Ronald B. Numbers (The Expositor's Bible Commentary) (Kindle Locations 6836-6840). Zondervan. Kindle Edition.
6. Allen, Ronald B. Numbers (The Expositor's Bible Commentary) (Kindle Locations 7085-7090). Zondervan. Kindle Edition.
7. Allen, Ronald B. Numbers (The Expositor's Bible Commentary) (Kindle Locations 7105-7106). Zondervan. Kindle Edition.

TWO
WHO WAS BALAAM?

A line of ants traveled up and down Balak's back. He was afraid. His enemies in the north, Og and Sihon—enemies he had struggled with unsuccessfully for years—had been swiftly destroyed by a new people. Rumors had spread that these Israelites worshipped a god who had destroyed the entire land of Egypt with disaster after disaster. These former slaves had strong magic through their deity, Yahweh.

Balak looked out over the fragile grassland of Moab. Like a herd of voracious oxen devouring grass this people would devour their land. He didn't have the military strength to overcome the Amorites, let alone this new enemy who had routed so many enemies. He needed supernatural help. He needed the best.

> So Balak the son of Zippor, who was king of Moab at that time, sent messengers to Balaam the son of Beor at Pethor, which is near the River in the land of the people of Amaw, to call him, saying, "Behold, a people has come out of Egypt. They cover the face of the earth, and they are dwelling opposite me. Come now, curse this people for me, since they are too mighty for me. Perhaps I shall be able to defeat them and drive them from the land, for I know that he whom you bless is blessed, and he whom you curse is cursed" (Numbers 22:1-6).

Balaam remains one of the most notorious characters in all the Bible, and though his story only spans from Numbers 22-24, his prophetic words endure as some of God's greatest promises to Israel and an everlasting prophecy of the coming Messiah. Balaam is mentioned by name in Deuteronomy, Joshua, Nehemiah, Micah, 2 Peter, and Jude, and Jesus references him by name in the Book of Revelation. In every mention after Balaam first appears in Numbers 22-24 he is universally condemned and stands as the archetypal false teacher or prophet.

You are probably reading this book because you want to be a servant of God. You may seek God's wisdom in discovering your calling, hearing God's voice, becoming a man or woman of character, finding God's message, or discovering your own prophetic gift or calling. Studying Balaam's life and what God continues to speak through it will help you discover all these things.

There is a reason the Old Testament and the New Testament point to Balaam again and again. There's a reason Peter and Jude refer to Balaam's ways as a familiar pattern of false teaching and evil character. There's a reason that Jesus in the Book of Revelation calls out Balaam's error as something to watch out for and repent of in these last days. And there is a reason that all of these warnings exist in spite of Balaam's accurate prophecies.

Balaam has been the subject of study and preaching since his first appearance in Scripture. Many have argued that he was either a good prophet who went bad or a bad prophet who experienced a moment of God's grace. To understand Balaam's story, it is important to begin with his origins and understand the biblical world from where Balaam emerges. Balaam was not a part of Israel's journey through the wilderness. Balaam comes out of the darkness of pagan culture and enters God's story of redemption as an opponent of Israel.

Balaam's own journey and how he came to be an internationally known spiritual powerhouse is shrouded in mystery. *The Transcription of Deir Alla* praises Balaam's abilities as truly legendary but remains obscure even to modern scholarship.

For this study of Balaam, it's important to realize that how we end is often determined by how we begin. What's more encouraging for us though, is that though Balaam encountered Israel's God late in life and late in his spiritual development, God gave him the opportunity to proclaim prophecies that would be read for millennia and truly stand forever as God's eternal word.

So how did Balaam begin? And more importantly, how should we?

Balaam clearly spoke God's Word by supernatural power. Balaam clearly saw into the spiritual realm. Balaam had an international reputation for accurate and effective supernatural ministry. However, the Bible never calls Balaam a prophet or a seer.

Part of this is because Balaam was not a Hebrew and didn't start out as a Hebrew prophet. Balak didn't come to Balaam because Balaam was a Hebrew prophet. He came to Balaam because Balaam was a spiritualist from within Balak's worldview and people group. He was a Mesopatamian Baru—a practitioner of divination and magic.[1]

> The sons of Israel also killed Balaam the son of Beor, the diviner, with the sword among the rest of their slain (Joshua 13:22 NASB).

We will revisit the question of whether Balaam ended up a true prophet, a false prophet, or a prophet at all again later, but when Balaam's story started, Balaam was a pagan diviner, not a prophet within Israel's prophetic tradition.

Balaam the Diviner

Ancient Near Eastern people believed in a pantheon of gods and goddesses. These gods had different traits and different domains. Some gods were bound by geography or only had specific abilities. One of the temptations the Israelites faced as they settled in new land was the belief that a new god ruled over the new land and that they could find prosperity by worshipping these new geographically centered gods.

Other gods were seen as more foundational to the world. When Jonah was trying to flee from Yahweh, the sailors who were conducting him away from Nineveh ran into a divinely inspired storm. They roughly woke Jonah demanding that he pray to his god. They didn't think about the true god or the false god. They believed there were many. They simply wanted him to appeal to whichever deity might help them.[2]

As the storm continued they began to think that the storm was because one of the gods was angry at one of them. It's unclear how they determined this. Perhaps they used divination themselves. They certainly weren't far off in their assessment. God was angry—with Jonah.

They cast lots to determine who God was angry at. I do not believe casting lots (or flipping a coin, or drawing straws) is divination, but we will discuss how to discern divination in the next chapter. The lot fell on Jonah, and he confessed his sin:

> And he said to them, "I am a Hebrew, and I fear the Lord, the God of heaven, who made the sea and the dry land." Then the men were exceedingly afraid and said to him, "What is this that you have done!" For the men knew that he was fleeing from the presence of the Lord, because he had told them (Jonah 1:9-10).

The sailors were terrified because Jonah confessed to not worshipping or belonging to any god, but to the Creator God, the greatest god in the pantheon. This god was seen as the most powerful and, depending on the religion, the farthest away from humanity. This god was not to be trifled with.[3]

Gods were not only territorial, but they could be influenced and manipulated by human activity. Through sacrifice, ritual magic, cutting oneself, or other activities; diviners could discern the will of the gods and appeal to the gods to act on their behalf. A skilled diviner was thought to be able to appeal to the right god and cause that god to act on the diviner's behalf. Sorcery, spell casting, and cursing brought the power of the gods to bear on one's situation. Or on one's enemies.[4]

We have an acute illustration of this in Elijah's showdown with the prophets of Baal. The prophets of Baal attempted to gain Baal's intervention to send fire and set the sacrifice aflame. They began shouting. Perhaps they shouted prayers, but it seems likely that they were also shouting spells or incantations. Elijah goads them on:

At noon Elijah began to taunt them. 'Shout louder!' he said. 'Surely he is a god! Perhaps he is deep in thought, or busy, or traveling. Maybe he is sleeping and must be awakened.' So they shouted louder and slashed themselves with swords and spears, as was their custom, until their blood flowed. Midday passed, and they continued their frantic prophesying until the time for the evening sacrifice. But there was no response, no one answered, no one paid attention" (1 Kings 18:27-29).

The prophets were whipping themselves into an ecstatic frenzy as they prophesied and cut themselves. Ecstatic experiences were thought to activate spells and personal desire into the spiritual realm. These prophets were attempting to activate and give power to their prophetic declarations through their own blood and ecstatic raving.[5] It didn't work. But a single prayer from Elijah to Yahweh brought fire from heaven.

Diviners used omens and different forms of divination to first discover the will of the gods or their plan for the future. Divination usually resulted from reading seemingly random patterns. Tarot cards are a form of divination that is easily recognizable today. The cards are shuffled and flipped over randomly, but then read and interpreted as if the pattern was instructive about the future. This can also be done by interpreting patterns in smoke, ripples in water, the patterns of birds, the position of the stars (astrology), or the characteristics of the liver in a slaughtered animal. This last method seems to be Balaam's preferred method of divination, but Ancient

Near Eastern texts also state that Balaam had encounters with the gods through dreams and visions.[6]

We will examine divination more in the next chapter and how it relates to our lives and even infiltrates the church today.

Balak's Way to Power

Balak wasn't seeking general advice or help from Balaam. He had a specific plan in mind. He would pay Balaam to curse his enemies.

Balak had a plan for how this should go. He would pay Balaam the appropriate price and provide the material for divination; in this case animals for sacrifice and liver reading. Balaam would then use these sacrifices to obtain power from the appropriate gods for an effective curse. In Balak's mind, he wasn't asking for someone to tell the future or divine the gods' will. He believed Balaam had the ability to manipulate the gods and use blessing and cursing power as he wished.[7]

Ancient Near eastern people believed in the power of the spoken word, and Balak used a form of the Hebrew word for "curse" three times in verse six. Curses were viewed as pronouncements that bound magical forces and constrained the gods to bring about the consequences of the curse. They were viewed as automatically fulfilled unless another force opposed or annulled them.[8]

You may think that this is a completely backward and evil way to see the world. Truly, Yahweh is neither bound nor constrained by curses or blessings. No pattern of words, no sacrifice, no act of ritual can bind or manipulate him. But have you ever tried to persuade God to do something for you by saying the right words? Have you ever tried to manipulate God through fasting? The Ancient Near Eastern ways may not be as far from us as we think.

Bruce Wilkinson's *The Prayer of Jabez* is one of the bestselling Christian books of all time, and may be the most popular example of this. *The Prayer of Jabez* is centered around a simple principle. If we ask God to bless us, He will. This is true. God is a good Father who gives good gifts to His children. And He loves it when we ask. If *The Prayer of Jabez* encourages you to believe in and ask for God's blessing, then you have received it properly.

However, if we believe that *reciting a specific prayer as a ritual* will access God's power and blessing, we may be entering the realm of magic and spiritual manipulation.

> And when you pray, do not heap up empty phrases as the Gentiles do, for they think that they will be heard for their many words (Matthew 6:7).

God wants to bless us through our relationship with Him. He wants us to ask for His blessing. But if we have no interest in relationship and simply go through a pattern of words or a pattern of steps to get God to do something for us we are at best immature. God wants us to grow up into Him and realize that everything we need is ours through Him (All that we need for life and godliness). Not through a ritual or a prayer.

Human beings are so tempted to believe that we can access spiritual power through our methods or our work. We think that if we just pray the right way we will get what we want. Or that if we pray enough or with enough fervency. We think that if follow the right pattern or method we will see miraculous healing because we do it the "right way."

I firmly believe that one of the reasons Jesus used so many different methods to heal people is so that we wouldn't fall into this snare. We don't access power through a mechanical process. We can't manipulate the Holy Spirit or the power of God. We won't be blessed or used by God because we follow a pattern or ritual as if these actions contain the way to access power. We access God's power according to His will and by grace through faith. That means He gives us power and miracles we don't deserve when we walk in trust and obedience with Him. God is not moved by methods. But He is moved by relationship.

Moving the Gods

Balaam seems to have had a more complex view of spirituality than Balak. He truly believed that his power came from the deities he interacted with. He didn't see himself as possessing power to curse or bless on his own, instead he saw his power coming according to the will of the appropriate god.[9]

If Balaam was called upon to bless Midian's crops, he would have used divination to ascertain the activity in the pantheon of gods and perhaps discover that the land was infertile because Asherah, known as the "Queen of Heaven" wasn't blessing the land. He would then take part in a sacrifice and ritual that would gain Asherah's favor and the sanction to bless Midian's crops from her supernatural ability.

Balaam seems to have seen his role primarily as an oracle, closer to a prophet than a sorcerer. He was more concerned with discerning the will of the gods and acting on their behalf. He had more respect for the gods and their abilities than Balak did, but as the story unfolds, it becomes clear that Balaam was used to having his way. In his experience, the gods could be manipulated.

Today's Gods

While many express faith in spiritual beings and powers, few people today view the world the way Balak, Balaam, and the Ancient Near Eastern people did. Science has disabused us of the notion that the spiritual world is a struggle between various gods in a pantheon. Many see polytheists and magic practitioners as silly or superstitious.

The Corinthian church worshipped the one true God in the midst of a culture that was swimming with different gods.

Idols and sacrifices to idols were so prevalent that it grieved Paul, and issues from coming out of idolatry and living in an idolatrous culture plagued the church. Paul was clear with the Corinthians that there is no God but one:

> We know that "An idol is nothing at all in the world" and that "There is no God but one." 5 For even if there are so-called gods, whether in heaven or on earth (as indeed there are many "gods" and many "lords"), 6 yet for us there is but one God, the Father, from whom all things came and for whom we live; and there is but one Lord, Jesus Christ, through whom all things came and through whom we live (1 Corinthians 8:4b-6).

Idols are not real. There are no other gods. But that doesn't mean that there aren't warring spiritual beings in the spiritual realm. Or that these beings don't get involved in the idolatry, divination, and spiritual manipulation of human beings.

> No, but the sacrifices of pagans are offered to demons, not to God, and I do not want you to be participants with demons. You cannot drink the cup of the Lord and the cup of demons too; you cannot have a part in both the Lord's table and the table of demons (1 Corinthians 10:20-21).

Paul is clear that demons, evil spiritual beings, do become involved in the worship and appeal to false gods. Just because idols are not real, and gods like Poseidon don't exist, does not mean that these activities are superstitious behavior that have no result or spiritual value. The Ancient Near Eastern people practiced divination and magic because in their experience *it worked*. Satan and the demons were happy to receive the worship these people reserved for their gods. And Satan and the demons are willing to demonstrate and use some of their agency and ability on behalf of people if it would gain them the person's heart and allow their power and influence to spread through the culture.

In Balak's mind, he was asking Balaam to curse the people of Israel using the spiritual power Balaam had access to. In Balaam's mind, he was discovering the will of the gods through divination, accessing their power through magic, and releasing their power according to their will in blessings and curses.

From God's perspective Balak was asking Balaam to access demonic power to curse Israel.

God saw the larger cosmic war that raged over Israel and humanity. Satan knew that God had promised a Savior would be born from a human female, and that this Savior would crush Satan.[10] Satan had been attempting to corrupt and destroy humanity from the face of the earth from that time on. He used different strategies and methods, but Satan's desire was to destroy humans and prevent the Savior from coming. When God made a promise to Abraham that he would multiply his descendants and bless the world through them,

Satan turned his attention to destroying Abraham's descendants and the people of Israel.

The slavery of Egypt and the conflict with Pharaoh was a heavenly battle between God's plan to bring the Savior through Israel and Satan's desire to destroy and enslave the nation of Israel. The showdown between Moses and the Egyptian sorcerers and their gods, every battle during the journey through the desert, and every temptation in the wilderness was part of the adversary's attempts to derail the eternal plan of God for the redemption of humanity. Satan wanted to stop the ultimate arrival of the Jesus Christ, salvation, and the gospel.

Balak's attempt to curse Israel through Balaam was one more attempt by the adversary to destroy Israel and prevent the arrival of the Savior. But God had other plans. Balaam was about to discover that Yahweh could not be compared to the other gods he served.

---

1. Allen, Ronald B. Numbers (The Expositor's Bible Commentary) (Kindle Locations 9843-9844). Zondervan. Kindle Edition.
2. Walton, John H. Jonah (The Expositor's Bible Commentary) (p. 472). Zondervan.
3. Ibid.
4. Zondervan. 2016. NIV Cultural Backgrounds Study Bible: New International Version. (p. 268). Zondervan.
5. Heschel, Abraham Joshua. The Prophets, II. P.133-134. Prince Press.
6. T. Witton Davies, Magic, Divination and Demonology Among the Hebrews and Their Neighbors (reprint of 1898 ed.; New York: Ktav Publishing House, Inc., 1969), p 75.

7. Van Imschoot, Paul. Theology of the Old Testament (trans. Kathryn Sullivan and Fidelis Buck; Tournai: Desclee & Co., 1965), 1: 189–90 quoted in Allen, Ronald B. Numbers (The Expositor's Bible Commentary) (Kindle Locations 9923-9924). Zondervan. Kindle Edition.
8. U. Cassuto (A Commentary on the Book of Genesis [trans. Israel Abrahams; Jerusalem: Magnes Press, The Hebrew University, 1961, 1964], 2: 155) quoted in Allen, Ronald B. Numbers (The Expositor's Bible Commentary) (Kindle Locations 9931-9932). Zondervan. Kindle Edition.
9. Allen, Ronald B. Numbers (The Expositor's Bible Commentary) (Kindle Locations 10039-10041). Zondervan. Kindle Edition.
10. Genesis 3:15.

THREE
DEFINING DIVINATION

I sat in a tiny living room drinking coffee with my friend Marco and his mother. Marco is Albanian. I enjoyed Turkish coffee, and Marco's mom was happy to make it for me. She loved it that Marco had a friend who was so focused on God. She was a devout Catholic, and the living room was decorated with portraits of Jesus and Mary. Turkish coffee keeps the grounds in the cup and they form a think sludge at the bottom. Marco's mom finished her coffee before I did and deftly flipped the cup upside down on the saucer. When Marco finished he also flipped the cup upside down quickly without sloshing any liquid or grounds.

I was getting used to cross cultural ministry and thought, "when in Rome..." I finished my coffee and flipped the cup upside down on the saucer as well. Marco burst out laughing.

"No, no... you don't have to do that." Both he and his mother laughed and then became slightly embarrassed. "This is just something we [meaning Albanians] do. It's to get your fortune." Both he and his mother were embarrassed as they explained that this was on old tradition. After the grounds slid down the side of the upturned cup and settled, they would flip the cup back over and read the pattern of the grounds to discern the future.

They seemed bashful, and Marco's mother explained, "We really shouldn't do it." For some reason they both had an instinct that it was either wrong or silly.

"If you talk to God," I said, "He can tell you your future much better." They both agreed.

As innocuous as it seems, what Marco and his mother were doing by reading the grounds at the bottom of the coffee cup was divination.

Defining Divination

> Divination may be provisionally defined as the attempt on man's part to obtain from the spiritual world supernormal or superhuman knowledge. This knowledge relates for the most part to the future, but it may also have to do with things in the present, such as where some hidden treasure is to be found. Divination takes for granted the primitive belief that spiritual beings exist, are approachable by man, have means of

knowledge which man has not, and are willing upon certain conditions known to diviners to communicate the special knowledge which they are believed to possess.[1]

In the seminal scholarly work on the subject, T. Witton Davies goes on to say that divination was originally a method of consulting the gods. Divination came out of an inherently polytheistic worldview.[2] It wasn't simply attempting to tell the future but using methods to consult and communicate with the gods.

Few people in our culture are polytheistic, but the principles behind divination remain the same. Diviners initiate methods to consult spiritual power or powers to discover hidden knowledge about the past, present, or future.

These days diviners usually do not ascribe this knowledge to the gods, but often to their own abilities to get information from an impersonal source like "the cosmos" or "universal energy." They may claim the information comes from a force, or that the information comes from the subconscious or the internal knowledge of one's DNA or body.

Whatever the source, divination is a process that depends on supernatural or unknown forces to reveal otherwise unknown information. It may claim to have a scientific basis, but divination is desirable specifically because it allows us to get information that natural observation cannot access. Some may even claim that the knowledge comes from the one true God.

JONATHAN AMMON

How Divination Works

Divination is not direct communication with deity. Divination finds information through some intermediary means and process. In other words, rather than hearing from God or a god (or demon) directly, the divine information must be received and interpreted through a phenomenon or method. Usually this involves reading and interpreting order or patterns in something that seems random, like how coffee grounds slide down the side of an upturned cup.

In ancient times diviners who sought supernatural knowledge would inscribe arrows with different signs or messages. They would then draw the arrows randomly or shoot them into the air with the one that landed closest to the target being the one that was supernaturally chosen.[3] Does this remind you of anything? Essentially this is just another form of the popular "Magic Eight Ball" toy. It provides a random way of selecting a message. The user applies or supplies faith that a supernatural force is choosing the message.

Another popular Near Eastern method was reading livers. The diviner would sacrifice animals to the gods and then read the features of the animals' livers to discover divine messages. This practice became sophisticated enough to produce diagrams and systems for interpretation.[4] The Hebrew words used to describe Balaam's activities in Numbers 22-24 most likely refer to this practice.[5]

Other methods mentioned in the Bible include Joseph's supposed divination chalice (Genesis 44:5, 15).[6] A diviner would drop a stone into the cup of water and the pattern of the ripples could be read as a message. Astrology also comes up frequently. The movement of the stars and the planets was unpredictable and produced a wealth of information that could be interpreted as messages from supernatural forces. The flight patterns of birds and other omens were believed to have supernatural significance. All of these methods require both initiating and interpreting phenomena and don't start with God's revelation, but with human intention to find information from an impersonal source.

Today we see many similar and obvious forms of divination in palm reading, crystal balls, Ouija boards, reading tea leaves, and tarot cards.[7] Many less obvious forms have infiltrated our culture and even the lives of many believers.

A more obviously sinister form of divination involved necromancy or summoning the spirits or ghosts of the dead to communicate the will of the gods. The witch at Endor used this form of divination for Saul. Many may believe that this kind of divination only exists in horror movies, but I've read a Christian book that encouraged believers to summon their dead relatives in their imaginations in order to speak with them about past emotional wounds. The information these relatives gave them in their spontaneous imaginative communication was believed to be revelatory about heart conditions and the subconscious state. I believe that this, too, is necromancy.

How Do We Tell the Difference?

The difference between a prophet and a diviner is one of both principle and method. The prophet communicates directly with God. The diviner initiates a method to discover what God is saying. In ancient times both diviners and prophets communicated with Yahweh, but diviners used impersonal and methodological means. They sought revelation by initiating and reading a random pattern.

Some people believe that if a Christian is involved in the practice and the practice is done in the name of Jesus, then it is permitted. They believe that they could pray in the name of Jesus for revelation and then flip over tarot cards to discover God's will. But this is not waiting on God or discerning His voice. This is reading His will in impersonal objects. This is not how God desires us to know Him, and it opens us up to misusing spiritual power, or even accessing demonic power.

The tarot card example should be obvious, but many other situations are less obvious. There are many methods of divination and new ones pop up all the time. Rarely are these methods truly new, they are usually old methods dressed up in new or scientific language. We should ask the following questions:

- Who or what are we seeking for revelation?
- Is this knowledge being acquired through natural means (science, observation)?
- If we are openly and clearly seeking supernatural revelation, are we seeking this revelation from God through Jesus?
- And then finally, are we using a non-relational method of communication to receive this information?
- Are we reading and interpreting God's will from some phenomena outside of God?

What complicates things further is that several ways of hearing God's voice can be used in a manner that may seem similar to divination.

Signs

When Gideon heard the voice of God, he sought confirmation through miraculous signs.[8] God answered his prayer and gave him the signs he desired, but discerning God's will through a fleece is hardly relational. What's the difference between seeking and reading signs and divination? The answer isn't always clear.

Gideon sought confirmation through signs. He had already heard God, but he wanted to make sure he was hearing accurately and sought confirmation through a more objective means—an outside means. I believe that God honored and will honor this desire, but I often try to dissuade people from seeking signs, especially as a primary way of hearing God. Signs should be used for confirmation—the way Gideon used them. Even then, I've seen signs point people in the wrong direction. It is so easy for us to interpret things in a way that pleases our natural desires.

I remember asking God if I should ask a certain girl out on a date when I was single. Romance and finding a mate can be one of the hardest areas to hear God because we are often so emotional. This is why it's important to seek wise council from leaders and family. I felt strongly that God told me not to ask the girl out on a date. But I was lonely, and I thought she had good character *and* might match my calling. I asked God for a sign, and as I was driving in downtown Detroit I saw a street sign related to this girl's last name. *It's a sign!* I thought. But deep down I knew that this was wrong. I felt disturbed, upset, and confused. What was the Lord telling me? As I pursued the idea, it became clear that this "sign" was *not* the Lord speaking.

I could recount story after story from friends and acquaintances who pursued certain relationships, jobs, ministries, or activities because of a "sign," only to end up misled and in disaster. Our minds tend to find meaning and interpret signs that will please us and give us what our hearts desire. I would advise using signs sparingly and only as a way to confirm what you already believe you may be hearing from God.

Dreams

The Bible is full of God speaking through dreams and visions, but dreams and visions were also used in the practice of divination.[9] God mentions lying dreams and visions among the false prophets of Zechariah and Jeremiah's day,[10] and religious leaders from Muhammed to Joseph Smith have claimed supernatural revelation from God through dreams and visions. How can we tell the false from the true? How can we be sure that we are handling dreams properly?

The power of dreams is that they are usually outside of our influence and guidance. Scientists say that we dream every single night, but most of us only remember a fraction of our dreams. The fact that the false prophets had false and lying dreams lets us know that not all dreams are from God. Clearly nightmares and false dreams come from the enemy. Some dreams rise out of our own concerns and worries. But some dreams are from God.

We need to use the same basic forms of discernment when it comes to dreams that we use when it comes to other ways that God may speak (1 Thessalonians 5:21, 1 Corinthians 14:29).[11]

- Does this glorify God?
- Does this dream correspond to Scripture (2 Timothy 3:16-17)?
- Will this dream bear good fruit in my life?

- Can I sense God speaking directly through this dream? Or is it an indecipherable mix of images and symbols?

And so on.

Some ministers teach that every single dream is spiritual and that every single dream comes from God. I believe this is dangerous teaching. At best, it would bog us down with an immense amount of complex dream interpretation focusing on symbols and obscure messages. At worst it is stretching for a message from God that's not there or trying to use dreams as material for divination.

Spiritual dreams can be a great gift from God. He will let you know if a dream is from Him. Let Him speak to you and let any dream or phenomena draw you into His presence and create intimacy with Him where He speaks to you directly. Don't try to apply a pattern or system of interpretation to every single dream, straining for spiritual information that God isn't giving.

Objects in Prophecy

What about using objects in prophecy? Jeremiah used both a girdle and a yoke as object lessons during prophecy, is that divination?[12] In both cases Jeremiah used these objects to illustrate what God was saying. They were a picture of what

God was telling him. The objects weren't read or used to gain a message from God. They were illustrations.

Prophetic illustrations are clearly biblical, but using objects in prophecy can blur into divination. I remember an infamous controversy where a famous minister wrote a blog post about using tuning forks to prophesy. I'm not sure that I know what the author's intention was and cannot judge. It's possible that the tuning fork was being used as an illustration. It's also possible that they were being used to discern something. Randomly selecting tuning forks and reading or interpreting the different tones as a divine message can be a method of divination, in the same way as reading coffee grounds or ripples in water.

We need to be careful that we aren't trusting any object or pattern to reveal information. God is the revealer of secrets.[13] We want to hear God's voice, not discern information through objects.

Infiltration

While I am hesitant to judge situations without specific knowledge and the help of the Holy Spirit, I do believe that the charismatic movement and the natural and homeopathic medicine that is popular among many believers contain questionable practices and divination.

Charismatics are rightfully eager to prophesy.[14] But in our eagerness, we can rejoice in wrong methods of receiving revelation. We may feel justified because of their purpose: reaching the lost or sharing God's love. We may feel that because these methods seem to work, they must be God. But just because something seems to work or bless us in some way does not mean that they aren't wrong, harmful, or misleading. God blesses those who are sincerely seeking Him (Titus 1:15), and He often uses bad things to bless those who love Him.

We may feel that if we pray in Jesus's name we "sanctify" any method we may use, but that method can't justify other sins like sexual immorality. It can't justify divination either.

Homeopathic medicine borrows many techniques from Eastern medicine and religion, including dubious methods of diagnosis. Regardless of scientific or metaphysical language, any method that involves communicating with a substance or with the patient's body is suspect. Asking the body questions and reading responses; directing, reading, or using energies; or using spiritual discernment to communicate with medicines, oils, or supplements should raise red flags for believers.[15]

That is not to say that using anthropomorphic language or speaking about objects, parts of our bodies, or animals as if they were people is wrong. We often "talk" to our pets, our plants, and other objects. When we speak this way we aren't reading or expecting spiritual or metaphysical responses the way an energy healer or a crystal reader does.

Jesus and Using Spiritual Power

There aren't easy answers to some of these questions, which is why it is important for us to develop discernment. Since the garden we have yearned for a knowledge of good and evil. We want it laid out for us, and we want to have rules for ourselves. God gave the people rules on the mountain, and He forbid divination, but we still have to depend on His leading in each specific moment in order to discern good and evil, right and wrong. The Bible reinforces basic morality, but in order to apply it we need the help of the Holy Spirit.

And Jesus, full of the Holy Spirit, returned from the Jordan and was led by the Spirit in the wilderness 2 for forty days, being tempted by the devil. And he ate nothing during those days. And when they were ended, he was hungry. 3 The devil said to him, "If you are the Son of God, command this stone to become bread." 4 And Jesus answered him, "It is written, 'Man shall not live by bread alone.'" (Luke 4:1-4)

Satan tempted Jesus to use spiritual power to turn stones into bread. Jesus was God in the flesh—the Son of God. Why would Satan tempt Him to turn stones into bread? Why would it be wrong? Jesus turned water into wine. He multiplied bread and fish. Why shouldn't he turn stones into bread? This was a situation where Jesus needed to know God's will in order to discern right from wrong. But Jesus clearly knew that this would be wrong and responded to Satan accordingly. His response reveals a powerful principle for all of us today.

Jesus could do anything. He was omnipotent. He could use His universe-creating power at any time. But He didn't. In order to fulfill His purpose on earth He had to let go of His heavenly power and live and minister on earth not as the glorified God, but as a human being in perfect relationship with God the Father.[16]

Satan was tempting Jesus to not rely on the Father and His will, but to use His own power for himself. Satan was tempting Jesus to use spiritual power outside of relationship with the Father. What we learn from this is the principle that can keep us safe in all of our experiences with spiritual power.

Never use spiritual power outside of intimate relationship with and dependency on God.

Rely on Him. It is better to fail than try to use spiritual power in your own strength. It is better to be embarrassed or to disappoint others than to summon up something within yourself. Whatever you do, do in relationship with the Father. Do all things by His power and ability.

> By myself, I can do nothing (John 5:30).

I believe that human beings do have some measure of spiritual power and activity within themselves. When God breathed His breath into us He created us with a human spirit that had some of the divine life and eternal spark of God. Without it, none of us would be alive or conscious. We would be like the animals. Human beings were made in the image of God. We are spiritual beings created with spiritual abilities that are meant to come alive in our relationship—and *only* in our relationship—with God.

It is possible to exercise some kinds of spiritual power without either God or demons. Human beings are spiritual beings and can act and discern in the spiritual realm. Some people are born with more spiritual sensitivity than others, and can learn to engage in spiritual activity. But this spiritual activity is forbidden. It is dangerous.[17]

One of the reasons people are tempted by divination and use it is because it works. Divination applied correctly can access spiritual power. That spiritual power may come from an individual's own latent spiritual gift or intuition or it may come from demons, but either way it crosses the line.

It may accurately reveal the future or it may deceive. Even if it provides an accurate result, it is wrong. God will not be manipulated, and He wants us to seek His wisdom and knowledge alone.

Divination is always wrong. Asking God for wisdom and knowledge is always right.[18]

God Forbids Divination

> When you come into the land that the Lord your God is giving you, you shall not learn to follow the abominable practices of those nations. There shall not be found among

> you anyone who burns his son or his daughter as an offering, anyone who practices divination or tells fortunes or interprets omens, or a sorcerer or a charmer or a medium or a necromancer or one who inquires of the dead, for whoever does these things is an abomination to the Lord. And because of these abominations the Lord your God is driving them out before you. You shall be blameless before the Lord your God, for these nations, which you are about to dispossess, listen to fortune-tellers and to diviners. But as for you, the Lord your God has not allowed you to do this (Deuteronomy 18:9-14).

God expressly forbid His people from tolerating anyone who practiced divination, and He was clear that this was not only something that separated Israel from other nations like dietary restrictions, but a sin that God judged foreign nations for practicing.

In 1 Samuel 15:23 God calls divination a sin. In 2 Kings 17:17 He says that it's a sin that provokes His anger. In Ezekiel and Jeremiah God continually characterizes divination as "false," "lying," "flattering," and deceptive.[19]

> And the Lord said to me: "The prophets are prophesying lies in my name. I did not send them, nor did I command them or speak to them. They are prophesying to you a lying vision, worthless divination, and the deceit of their own minds (Jeremiah 14:14).

> My hand will be against the prophets who see false visions and who give lying divinations. They shall not be in the council of my people, nor be enrolled in the register of the house of Israel, nor shall they enter the land of Israel. And you shall know that I am the Lord God (Ezekiel 13:9).

In Acts 16 Paul casts a demon or "spirit of divination" out of a woman. The ability to practice divination can come at the cost of demonization. God wants what is best for us. His supernatural leadership provides all the guidance, wisdom, and knowledge we need. All supernatural or spiritual guidance outside of relationship with God through Jesus Christ is forbidden and harmful to the believer.

Pursuing God's Voice with a Clear Conscience

The burden of this chapter is to correct the practice of divination within the Church, and encourage everyone to hear from God as directly and personally as possible. I want to make sure that these corrections do not strike the tender-hearted with the fear of approaching God the wrong way. God loves you, and He wants to speak to you. If you approach hearing God with a pure heart and sincerely seek to follow His Word, you can feel safe in hearing His voice. He will not condemn you.

> To the pure, all things are pure, but to the defiled and unbelieving, nothing is pure; but both their minds and their consciences are defiled (Titus 1:15).

I am concerned for those who desire the miraculous and desire spiritual power and activity more than they desire to grow in direct relationship with God. Divination is wrong. Initiating and interpreting a random or varied phenomenon to hear from God is wrong. But that doesn't mean that all interpretation is wrong. There are many Scriptures about interpreting tongues, interpreting dreams, and interpreting symbols in God's revelation.

Getting supernatural or spiritual messages from crystals is wrong. But that doesn't mean that God doesn't speak through nature. All of nature testifies of God's attributes (Romans 1:20) and God can use events in nature like the earthquake in Acts 4:31 to speak to us.

We should approach God in prayer with open hearts and allow Him to speak to us as He wills. You shouldn't initiate a method of interpretation to hear from God anymore than you should initiate a method of interpretation to hear from a friend or a spouse. Approaching God requires faith, we see through a dark glass now (1 Corinthians 13:12), but God is a Father who loves you and wants to speak to you directly of His own volition and in His own way.

Despite God's express ban on divination, sometimes He will answer the call of those seeking true spiritual guidance outside of relationship with Him. God is immensely merciful and compassionate to those who don't know him and constantly pursuing the lost. He pursued diviners and sorcerers throughout the Bible, and He pursues them today. He meets them where they are and in their sinful practices and promises them a new life with Christ who has all authority and all power.

But God doesn't want to meet us through sinful practice. He will and He can, but He wants to meet you in the righteousness of Christ at His throne where you can approach Him boldly, without intermediaries or practices of divination. You have access to God through Jesus Christ and can talk to Him like a Father.

God guided the magi of Jesus's time and testified to the magicians of Babylon through Daniel. He speaks today to drug users on acid trips, to Hindus in meditation, and to shaman casting spells.

He even reached out to a pagan diviner named Balaam who sought the Hebrew God through divination with a plan to curse God's people.

---

1. T. Witton Davies, Magic, Divination and Demonology Among the Hebrews and Their Neighbors (reprint of 1898 ed.; New York: Ktav Publishing House, Inc., 1969), p 6.
2. Merrill F. Unger, Biblical Demonology: A Study of the Spiritual Forces Behind the Present World Unrest (Wheaton, Ill.: Scripture Press, 1952), p. 120.

3. Ibid. p. 75
4. Zondervan. 2016. NIV Cultural Backgrounds Study Bible: New International Version. (p. 268). Zondervan.
5. Allen, Ronald B. Numbers (The Expositor's Bible Commentary) (Kindle Locations 10043). Zondervan. Kindle Edition.
6. T. Witton Davies, Magic, Divination and Demonology Among the Hebrews and Their Neighbors (reprint of 1898 ed.; New York: Ktav Publishing House, Inc., 1969), p 82.
7. 1 Samuel 28.
8. Judges 6.
9. Davies. P. 77
10. Jeremiah 23:32, Zechariah 10:2
11. The book *Voice of God* by Art Thomas, James Loruss, and myself features several important chapters on testing revelation and judging prophecy.
12. Jeremiah 13, Jeremiah 27
13. Daniel 2:47 NKJV
14. 1 Corinthians 14:39
15. This subject could fill a whole book and even then, would need to be updated constantly with new methods and medicines. I have appreciated many of Neil Anderson's books on sanctification and have browsed his book *The Biblical Guide to Alternative Medicine*. Those who want to read more on this subject may benefit from seeking out that book.
16. You must have the same attitude that Christ Jesus had.
    > Though he was God,
    > he did not think of equality with God
    > as something to cling to.
    > Instead, he gave up his divine privileges;
    > he took the humble position of a slave
    > and was born as a human being.
    > When he appeared in human form,
    > he humbled himself in obedience to God
    > and died a criminal's death on a cross. Philippians 2:5-8 NLT
17. An exploration of what the Bible says about spiritual power and its use deserves a whole book in itself. Western believers are used to a dualistic approach to spiritual power—all spiritual power either comes from God or Satan. However, the Bible's portrayal of the spiritual world is more

nuanced. I would argue that while all spiritual power and life ultimately comes from God, God has given Satan, demons, and human beings some amount of spiritual agency in this world. Spiritual power can come from God or Satan, but human beings possess some spiritual ability within themselves because of the image of God. I cannot quickly prove this, but I believe an investigation of the Scriptures will reveal that this view better explains spiritual activity than the dualistic view. The message of this book remains relevant whether you accept this view or not.

18. James 1:5.
19. See Ezekiel 12-13, 21; Micah 3.

FOUR
BALAAM MEETS YAHWEH

> So the elders of Moab and the elders of Midian departed with the fees for divination in their hand. And they came to Balaam and gave him Balak's message. And he said to them, "Lodge here tonight, and I will bring back word to you, as the Lord speaks to me." So the princes of Moab stayed with Balaam (Numbers 22:7-8).

Balak took action and sent a delegation made up of the elders of Moab and Midian to meet Balaam and hire him to curse Israel. He treated Balaam like a big shot. Balaam inspired fear in the king. Balak didn't send servants to summon Balaam. He sent leaders.

These elders carried the "fees for divination" in their hand. This is straightforward evidence that Balaam was a diviner and that his gift was for hire. Fees for divination were standard practice in the ancient world in the same way that psychics or tarot card readers operate for money today. Someone with Balaam's reputation could command a sizeable fee. In addition to payment to the diviner, fees for divination sometimes included sacrificial animals or equipment which would be used in the divination process.[1]

While it was normal for diviners to receive fees for their service at this time, it was also normal for prophets to receive fees for ministry as well. When Saul first met Samuel, his initial concern was that he did not have a gift to honor the prophet:

> Saul said to his servant, "If we go, what can we give the man? The food in our sacks is gone. We have no gift to take to the man of God. What do we have?"
>
> The servant answered him again. "Look," he said, "I have a quarter of a shekel of silver. I will give it to the man of God so that he will tell us what way to take." (Formerly in Israel, if someone went to inquire of God, they would say, "Come, let us go to the seer," because the prophet of today used to be called a seer.) (1 Samuel 9:7-9).

Prophetic ministry and money is a touchy subject. I first learned about prophets and prophetic ministry from a ministry culture that taught that only false prophets ever asked for money. On the other side of the spectrum, many are aware or a part of a culture that sells everything from recorded prophetic words to "Psalm 91 Protection Oil" blessed by a prophet.

We should maintain a culture that honors ministry and shares freely with those who invest the Word of God in our lives (Galatians 6:6). Ministers should freely give as they have freely received (Matthew 10:8). Samuel was not condemned by God for receiving money for his ministry, and at the end of his leadership he was vindicated by God for his integrity in finances. God was a witness between him and the people that he had defrauded no one (1 Samuel 12:1-5).

The short phrase "fees for divination" introduces themes that mark the rest of Balaam's story and his legacy. Balaam's story reveals a man who had the ability to demonstrate integrity in times of intense pressure. But it also reveals a man whose heart was consumed by greed.

> They have eyes full of adultery, insatiable for sin. They entice unsteady souls. They have hearts trained in greed. Accursed children! Forsaking the right way, they have gone astray. They have followed the way of Balaam, the son of Beor, who loved gain from wrongdoing, (2 Peter 2:14-16).
>
> Woe to them! For they walked in the way of Cain and abandoned themselves for the sake of gain to Balaam's error and perished in Korah's rebellion (Jude 1:11).

Balaam was motivated by greed. He wanted riches and honor. "The way of Balaam" and "Balaam's error" is seeking to get rich from sin or wrongdoing. Every time we twist the truth or compromise our morality for money we are making the same mistake Balaam made. Every time we cheat on our taxes, engage in business to promote something that God is not pleased with, or cheat our way to a greater income, we are compromising our souls for money.

I was once in a church service where the pastor began the offering time by asking the congregation, "How many of you would like to be rich?" About one third of the congregation raised their hands. He said, "The rest of you are liars." He went on to teach that God wanted His people to be rich and that God would financially bless individuals who gave.

I don't believe that God desires people to be poor, but the Scripture clearly says, "But those who desire to be rich fall into temptation, into a snare, into many senseless and harmful desires that plunge people into ruin and destruction" (1 Timothy 6:9). Maybe the congregation *was* lying, but the pastor was wrong to teach that we should all want to be rich or that it is okay to desire to be rich. This may not be a popular teaching, and "rich" varies from culture to culture, but if your heart is set on money you are running into destruction.

Balaam's greed misled him. Greed will mislead you too if you don't repent. Greed often gets an easy pass in our Christian culture, but it didn't in the New Testament. In 1 Corinthians the Bible says not to associate with people who claim to be Christians but are greedy (1 Corinthians 5:11) and that the greedy will not inherit the Kingdom of God (1 Corinthians 6:10). Greed and faith in Jesus are not compatible.

Greed is a hallmark of false teachers. They are motivated by money and extort God's people. Their desires are set on this world. Greed is not always easy to spot, especially in our wealthy culture. But God is clear that the greedy are disqualified from leadership in the body of Christ (Titus 1:7, 1 Timothy 3:8) and from the Kingdom of God (1 Corinthians 6:10).

Balaam's story is complex and reveals that he possessed several qualities we should admire. He heard God accurately and spoke God's Word. I wish all ministers of the gospel did so. I wish I always heard God accurately and spoke accurately. But Balaam's greed led him to disobey God in a major way.

Balaam wanted money, and he wanted to be paid. At the end of the story, that was his bottom line. As we will see later, he bent the rules and found a way to get paid. He thought he could outwit God and God's people. He succeeded in bringing one of the most powerful Messianic prophecies in the Bible, and introducing Israel to a sin that would plague them throughout history. His powerful words were not spoiled by his greed, but his ministry and his character were.

I have been in financially supported ministry since I graduated college. I've been both an itinerant minister and a missionary. I've handled money and ministry in different ways. When I started out I had a strong conviction to never ask for money. Later, when I got married and had a family to support, God released me from that conviction and taught me much more about money and ministry than I knew before. Either way, finances and ministry can be difficult and complex.

It is sin to be greedy or for ministry to be motivated by money. Those are inward heart issues that every servant of God must avoid. It is unethical to enrich yourself from ministry or fundraising.

But the workman is worthy of his hire (1 Timothy 5:18), and those who preach the gospel should make their living from the gospel (1 Corinthians 9:14). Those aren't opinions. That is Scripture.

Leaders who genuinely preach the gospel are worthy of financial support. Faithful elders should receive "double honor."[2] The Bible even says that ministers of the gospel have this as a "right.[3]" Ministers have the right or freedom to fundraise, and they have a right to make a living from their ministry work.

But this freedom should not be confused with greed or a desire to be rich. Money must never touch our hearts. Money must never be the ultimate motivation of our words or actions.

Even though Balaam stands out in the Bible as a false minister motivated by greed, his greed did not taint his prophecies about Israel, as we will see later.

BALAAM'S GOD

Balaam Seeks Yahweh

> And they came to Balaam and gave him Balak's message. And he said to them, "Lodge here tonight, and I will bring back word to you, as the Lord speaks to me." So the princes of Moab stayed with Balaam (Numbers 22:7-8).

Balaam accepted Balak's delegates, their message, and their fees for divination. He was open to receiving money for the task of cursing Israel. But he saw himself differently than Balak did. He did not believe that he could simply bless and curse who he wished. He believed he was bound to the powers and gods. He could only curse and bless from his ability to win the gods' favor or manipulate their action.[4]

Balaam told the delegates to wait alone for the night, and that in the evening he would ascertain whether or not he was able to curse Israel. He acted more like a prophet than a diviner from the start. He expected to hear a divine word and pass it on to the delegates. He planned to spend the night supernaturally hearing the voice of the divine.

Balaam had absolute confidence that he would receive an answer. Balaam's highly supernatural and spiritual worldview led him into an experience that was very different from ours. It was a false worldview, but pragmatically it was not as false as the naturalistic worldview that dominates our thinking today.

In Balaam's experience he could encounter any god and receive supernatural input from any deity with the right effort. The chance that a god would not answer didn't enter his mind. All gods were real, and all gods answered him. He applied his faith this way, and he got results.

He was still deceived. He was answered by demons and not by gods. But he tapped into the supernatural.

His confidence in the supernatural and his confidence in the reality of a God named Yahweh who worked on Israel's behalf led him to truly hear from Yahweh.

It is not clear how much Balaam knew about Yahweh. It seems likely that he had heard of Israel and their God. He probably believed that Yahweh was Israel's nationalistic deity and prepared to approach Yahweh in the same way he approached other gods.[5]

> The use of "Yahweh" in the mouth of the soothsayer is deemed significant. The redactor may have used it in order to make Balaam a true prophet. But another explanation, favored by our author, is that Balaam used "Yahweh" on purpose, just as he might have used the name of any other national deity. For it was on the basis of the call to the deity of the people that his curse would be more potent. Balaam would not have known that the god Yahweh was to be regarded any differently than any other "god."[6]

Since Yahweh was the God and protector of Israel, the director of Israel's fate, Balaam's beliefs demanded that he obtain the curse from Yahweh himself, not other gods. He would use divination and ritual to communicate with Yahweh and learn how to persuade and manipulate Yahweh into giving him the power to curse the people of Israel.

Balaam intended to meet Israel's deity. Instead, he started an encounter with the Creator of the universe.

Balaam's Conversation with Yahweh

> And God came to Balaam and said, "Who are these men with you?" (Numbers 22:9).

God initiated the encounter with Balaam. God spoke first, and as he spoke to Adam in sin in the garden, he spoke to Balaam in sin and asked a question.

> And Balaam said to God, "Balak the son of Zippor, king of Moab, has sent to me, saying, 'Behold, a people has come out of Egypt, and it covers the face of the earth. Now come, curse them for me. Perhaps I shall be able to fight against them and drive them out'" (Numbers 22:10-11).

Balaam answered God honestly. It is unclear at this point how he saw Yahweh. He may have been approaching Yahweh as just one more god he could manipulate, or he may have been aware that Yahweh would not easily go against His people Israel. It's also possible that God's voice in verse 9 shook Balaam.

> God said to Balaam, "You shall not go with them. You shall not curse the people, for they are blessed" (Numbers 22:12).

God unequivocally commanded Balaam not to go with the delegates and not to curse the people. He made His will clearly known. The people of Israel were irrevocably blessed. God would not allow Balaam to curse them.

Even though Balaam told the delegates that he had to seek the will of Yahweh, it seems likely that he did not expect this outcome. It may be that Balaam was simply paying lip service to God's will. He acted like the divine held the power and that he was an agent of the divine. But perhaps he actually he expected to have his way.

We often do the same thing. We pay lip service to God's sovereignty and reign in our lives. We tell others that we are bound by God's will. But many of us secretly or perhaps subconsciously expect to have our own way. We don't want God to intervene and change our plans.

Regardless of what Balaam's attitude may have been, he had the integrity to be honest about his encounter with Yahweh and told the delegates that he was not able to go with them.

> So Balaam rose in the morning and said to the princes of Balak, "Go to your own land, for the Lord has refused to let me go with you." So the princes of Moab rose and went to Balak and said, "Balaam refuses to come with us" (Numbers 22:13-14).

The conflict between the will of God, Balak's desire to curse Israel, and Balaam's desire to earn his fee began.

> So the Moabite officials returned to Balak and said, "Balaam refused to come with us."
>
> Then Balak sent other officials, more numerous and more distinguished than the first. They came to Balaam and said:
>
> "This is what Balak son of Zippor says: Do not let anything keep you from coming to me, because I will reward you handsomely and do whatever you say. Come and put a curse on these people for me."
>
> But Balaam answered them, "Even if Balak gave me all the silver and gold in his palace, I could not do anything great or small to go beyond the command of the Lord my God. Now spend the night here so that I can find out what else the Lord will tell me." (Numbers 22:14-19).

The Moabite officials did not report that God forbid Balaam from coming. Instead, they reported that Balaam refused to come. They did not hear God's voice for themselves, and while they clearly believed in Balaam's abilities, they either did not share his theology or simply did not believe that God had told him, "No." Balak didn't either.

The way Balak responded suggests that he did not believe that Balaam was really under a divine restriction. He believed Balaam was free to go where he chose. This was just a negotiation ploy for more money. He sent even higher ranking Moabite officials back to Balaam with an offer of a great reward. Balak didn't address the divine restriction; instead his shrewd response was "Do not let anything keep you from coming to me."

Few people really live as if their lives were directed by God. We tend to assume our freedom and do as we think best, praying that God will bless us. Balaam didn't do that. He stopped and asked God whether he could go or not. He wanted to be certain of God's power.

He asked for the wrong reasons—he wanted money. He asked out of insecurity— he wasn't in a covenant where God's power and blessing was promised. He asked out of ignorance—he didn't know God or God's plan. But he did ask.

We live in a covenant where relationship with God is promised. We live in a covenant where much of God's will is revealed. We don't have to ask, "Should I go and share the gospel with that person?" God has already told us to go and preach. He already promised that His power would accompany His word. This is why Paul so could so confidently and quickly move across the world. But God interrupted Paul often to tell him where to go and when. We have a command to go. God has revealed his general will in the Great Commission, but we still must submit to His guidance.

When was the last time you asked God whether you could go somewhere or do something? Do we really invite God into our decisions and seek His guidance? If we believe that God speaks to us, we should eagerly seek His input.

In spite of his greed and his desire for money, Balaam answered the Moabite officials with integrity.

> But Balaam answered them, "Even if Balak gave me all the silver and gold in his palace, I could not do anything great or small to go beyond the command of the Lord my God. Now spend the night here so that I can find out what else the Lord will tell me" (Numbers 22:18-19).

For someone who became the prototypical false teacher, Balaam had backbone. He wasn't a simple fraud prostituting his services to whoever would pay. He was genuinely attempting to be consistent in what he said and faithful to the source of his power.

What is even more interesting is that Balaam uses the word Yahweh here and calls Him, "my God." There are different interpretations of why Balaam speaks this way. While some suggest that Balaam is bragging about his familiarity with the Hebrew God, it is also possible that he is using emphasis. He is stating that he is under this God's power and command.

Yahweh has become his personal deity during this time, not just one god within a pantheon, but the God he serves.[7]

If this is true, it illuminates the story to come. For all his faults, Balaam did learn some powerful truths about the God of Israel. Truths that we often find difficult to learn. Unfortunately, like many, these truths did not ultimately touch Balaam's heart with the lasting love or the fear of the Lord.

Even though Balaam emphatically stated that he could do nothing unless the Lord commanded him, he did seek God again. He told the officials to wait and decided to ask God to let him go a second time. Have you ever asked God a question even though you knew the answer? Have you ever tried to get God to tell you something different than what He already told you?

I have many times, especially when I was single and asking God for a spouse. Even though God had spoken to me clearly, I would ask again and again. Not because I sincerely wanted to discover God's will, but because I wanted a wife soon. I didn't want to wait. I wanted God to change what he had told me previously. I kept my eyes out for "signs" that God had changed His mind and kept hoping I would hear something new.

I'm not the only one who makes this mistake. I have known many others who do the same thing. When we are in this mindset, we set ourselves up to be misled.

When God did lead me to Tatiana, my wife, He didn't use signs, visions, or dreams. He used a number of wise friends or counselors, an assurance in my heart, and a powerful word of encouragement from a friend. The Spirit led me to my wife through the prophetic community around me. I cannot tell you how much I grew from that process and how much joy I have in my covenant with Tatiana. Be patient for God's best.

Balaam sought God at night again with the same confidence as the last time he had heard God. I wonder how many of us, when we needed an answer from God would be confident enough to say, "I'm going to spend tonight seeking God. Tomorrow morning, I will have the answer." This was what Balaam was used to with other gods. Balaam had faith that God would answer. Balaam set aside considerable time to focus on hearing God. And whether he knew it or not, Balaam was in the middle of what God was interested in—Israel's journey. He met with God.

If we have positioned our lives to focus on what God is interested in, truly believe that God will answer, and set aside significant focused time to meet with Him—we will meet with God.

The Bible doesn't give us a full account of Balaam's encounter with God, but we know the result. The Bible informs us that Balaam continued to use divination to reach God until much later. His methods were based on manipulation. He was trying to bend God's will to his own, rather than trying to discover God's will.

Balaam must have felt successful. "That night God came to Balaam and said, 'Since these men have come to summon you, go with them, but do only what I tell you'" (Numbers 22:20). He may have even believed that he had successfully manipulated Yahweh. He would find out how wrong he was.

---

1. Cole, Dennis R. Numbers: An Exegetical and Theological Exposition of Holy Scripture: 3 (The New American Commentary) (Kindle Location 10901). B&H Publishing Group. Kindle Edition.
2. 1 Timothy 5:17
3. 1 Corinthians 9:1-12
4. Cole, Dennis R. Numbers: An Exegetical and Theological Exposition of Holy Scripture: 3 (The New American Commentary) (Kindle Location 10901). B&H Publishing Group. Kindle Edition.
5. Ibid. Kindle Location 10923.
6. Allen, Ronald Barclay. The Theology of the Balaam Oracles: A Pagan Diviner and the Word of God (Unpublished doctoral dissertation) p. 119. Dallas Theological Seminary, Dallas.
7. Cole, Dennis R. Numbers: An Exegetical and Theological Exposition of Holy Scripture: 3 (The New American Commentary) (Kindle Location 11002). B&H Publishing Group. Kindle Edition.

FIVE
BALAAM'S DONKEY

So Balaam rose in the morning and saddled his donkey and went with the princes of Moab (Numbers 22:21).

Even though God had expressly told him that he couldn't go with the princes of Moab or curse Israel in Numbers 22:12, Balaam tried a second time to get Yahweh to allow him to go. He wanted the honor and the reward Balak and the Moabites could give him. When God told Balaam he could go with them the second time, it was clear that he could only do so under the restriction that he would say what Yahweh told him to.

Balaam must have thought Yahweh had changed his mind. Maybe Yahweh was succumbing to Balaam's divination. Maybe the sacrifices and rituals were working. Balaam was traveling with the princes of Moab. He was one step closer to his honorarium.

We are all susceptible to hearing what we want to hear instead of what is said. This is as true in our relationship with God as it is with other people. We have our hearts so set on something we refuse to take "no" for an answer. If God says "no," we ask again. If God directs us elsewhere, we try to get a different word. Sometimes we even succeed.

When Israel desired a king, God clearly told the people through Samuel that it would be detrimental to them and that His plan was better. But they did not want to be led that way. They'd heard God clearly. A king was not God's best plan. They pressed on. They wanted what they wanted.

God gave them what they wanted, and the people's desire became part of God's plan as He spoke through Saul and David. But the people forfeited God's best. Who knows how Israel's history would have been different if they had been led by the priests and prophets instead of by the kings. "When that day comes, you will cry out for relief from the king you have chosen..." (1 Samuel 8:18a).

We can twist God's words to our own desires. God can speak clear and accurate words to individuals through prophecy. And those individuals can hear something completely different than what was said. They can twist interpretations to their own desires. They can torture Bible verses to fit their theology. They can find others who will confirm them in their error.

As ministers we can be susceptible to this, as well. We can pick up on people's desires and their projections. Rather than listening to what God is saying, we can read what the person's desire is and prophesy it back to them. We can value "revelation" or prophecy so highly that we would rather say something that we can discern than be sure that what we are saying is from the Lord. We can value producing prophecy more than we value caution or accuracy.

What's more, we want to say good words to people. We want people to *feel* blessed by our ministry. We want to say, "yes!" to their dreams and desires. But God often has a better plan than we realize.

We know that God loves us and wants our best. We know that God works within relationship with us, and that He often births dreams and visions within us. We know that God promises to give us the desires of our hearts if we delight in Him.

But we can't assume that God will say "yes" to every dream and every desire. We also can't assume that God will say yes to every desire we encounter in prophetic ministry. Sometimes it's easier to read people's intentions and desires than it is to hear from the Lord. Prophetic ministry can succeed on a surface level by telling people what they want to hear but drown in the desires of the people. We want words from God's heart.

David had a dream to build God's house—a temple for God. This was a good desire. David wanted to do something for God. He was anointed by God. He loved God and God's people. It was hard to imagine a better man for the project. David was careful; he asked Nathan the Seer if God would allow him to build the temple. Nathan saw how good the dream was. He saw how fitted David seemed to the task. He knew the temple was what God desired, too. He felt confident in confirming David's desire and told David to go for it (2 Samuel 7:3).

But that night God rebuked Nathan (2 Samuel 7:4-17). Even though David's desire was good, it was not God's plan. God had values Nathan and David didn't understand. God saw a greater perspective. He forbade David from building the temple because of David's participation in war. God promised that David's son Solomon would complete the temple. Sometimes God says "no" to our dreams. Even when they are to do wonderful things for His name.

David was disheartened, but he obeyed God. He went out of his way to complete the logistics so that Solomon would be prepared to build the temple. He took the role of a servant to the man who would be able to complete the vision.

David was truly a man after God's own heart. He had the humility and the obedience to release his dream and his desire. He had the grace to help serve those God would make successful in that area.

Each of us must examine our own hearts and our own desires. We must have an absolute commitment to the Word of God and a firm stance to say whatever God is saying regardless of the pressure of the community or the clear desires we sense coming from an individual.

David obeyed God and gave up his dream and desire, and God was pleased. I wonder what would have happened if David had not obeyed God. What if he had argued? What if he had said that the fact that he was a man of war wasn't a valid reason for why he couldn't build the temple. Hadn't God told him to fight those wars and battles? It must have felt like God wasn't being just to punish him for something that God made him do.

The story would have been very different if David had responded that way. It may have looked a little more like Balaam's story.

Balaam's Donkey and the Angel

> But God's anger was kindled because [Balaam] went, and the angel of the Lord took his stand in the way as his adversary. Now he was riding on the donkey, and his two servants were with him (Numbers 22:22).

Balaam knew what God wanted. God had spoken clearly to him, first to not go with the Moabites because Israel was blessed and not cursed. Balaam went to God again in an effort to bend God's will through magic, and God spoke again. This time telling Balaam to go, but cautioning him to not curse Israel but to speak what God commanded.

Balaam was happy to go with the Moabites. In his heart he thought he was making progress toward getting what he wanted. He was making friends and influencing gods. He would soon have his fee. God saw that his intention was to continue trying to manipulate his way into cursing Israel.

God is patient and compassionate. He met this pagan diviner where he was and spoke to him. He revealed His will to this man. But Balaam refused to repent or to turn away from his desire for money and his plan to get it through cursing Israel. God became angry and sent an angel to meet Balaam on the road.

> And the donkey saw the angel of the Lord standing in the road, with a drawn sword in his hand. And the donkey turned aside out of the road and went into the field. And Balaam struck the donkey, to turn her into the road (Numbers 22:23).

Even at this early time in history donkeys were seen much as they are today—stupid and stubborn.[1]

Though Balaam was famous for being able to see into the spiritual realm, in this instance, he was blind. He did not see the angel or the danger standing in his way. Balaam who used animals and animal organs to see and hear the divine, could not read his own donkey's behavior.

Then the angel of the Lord stood in a narrow path between the vineyards, with a wall on either side. And when the donkey saw the angel of the Lord, she pushed against the wall and pressed Balaam's foot against the wall. So he struck her again (Numbers 22:24-25).

Again the angel blocked Balaam's way, and again he was blind to what was happening.

> Then the angel of the Lord went ahead and stood in a narrow place, where there was no way to turn either to the right or to the left. When the donkey saw the angel of the Lord, she lay down under Balaam. And Balaam's anger was kindled, and he struck the donkey with his staff (Numbers 22:26-27).

The third and final time the angel confronted Balaam, he stood in a narrow place where Balaam could not turn aside. Balaam's donkey laid down and refused to move. In effect, she was trying to save her own life and the life of Balaam. Balaam lost his temper and hit her again.

And that's when God intervened and opened the mouth of the donkey.

> Then the Lord opened the mouth of the donkey, and she said to Balaam, "What have I done to you, that you have struck me these three times?" And Balaam said to the donkey, "Because you have made a fool of me. I wish I had a sword in my hand, for then I would kill you." And the donkey said to Balaam, "Am I not your donkey, on which you have ridden all your life long to this day? Is it my habit to treat you this way?" And he said, "No" (Numbers 22:28-30).

God is truly ruler of all creation, and like many of the events in the Balaam story this is a supernatural miracle. This is one of the sections that scholars struggle to accept and want to explain away. Some argue that this story is a later, mythical addition. I believe this is the Word of God and making a donkey speak doesn't seem any more miraculous than Jesus' resurrection from the dead, which we must believe to be saved.

There are several ways this miracle could have operated. The Bible clearly states that the Lord opened the mouth of the donkey. God caused the donkey to talk. 2 Peter 2:16 says that the donkey spoke with a human voice. Balaam was someone who read the will of the gods from animals, and this is comedic and a harsh rebuke to Balaam's pride.

The donkey's message itself is interesting. The donkey cried out in pain, to ask why Balaam was striking her. This was not a prophetic message from the Lord, but God supernaturally enabling the donkey to respond to Balaam in a way that Balaam understood. Balaam answered, seemingly without a second thought, expressing his anger. He didn't seem at all surprised that the animal spoke. Perhaps he was so overcome with anger that he didn't realize what was happening. Perhaps he was so used to the supernatural that it didn't shock him the way it does us. Or perhaps the biblical account simply leaves out his reaction.

Whatever surprise Balaam may have felt didn't stop him from being angry. He wished he had a sword in his hand. He did not know that another being stood before him with a sword ready to strike him.

The donkey responded to Balaam and spoke in the first person. Again, this wasn't the donkey prophesying or speaking a message from God. God was enabling the donkey to give a reasoned response to Balaam in a language he understood. This was part of God's convicting and humbling of the diviner.

The animal Balaam could have used as a tool for divination saw into the spiritual realm in a way Balaam did not and spoke from the power of God in a way that Balaam did not. God forced Balaam to be dependent on His power and His will. He was in the process of showing Balaam who was in control. The diviner had not manipulated Yahweh. Yahweh would use the diviner in His own plan.

> Then the Lord opened the eyes of Balaam, and he saw the angel of the Lord standing in the way, with his drawn sword in his hand. And he bowed down and fell on his face. And the angel of the Lord said to him, "Why have you struck your donkey these three times? Behold, I have come out to oppose you because your way is perverse before me. The donkey saw me and turned aside before me these three times. If she had not turned aside from me, surely just now I would have killed you and let her live" (Numbers 22:31-33).

Yahweh opened Balaam's eyes. We are also dependent on the Father for spiritual sight. We cannot gain the legitimate gift through books or seminars, rituals, activations, or any other method. God must give us the ability. Teaching and wisdom from others can help. That's part of what this book is about, but God is in control over who sees and who does not. Balaam learned that he was blind without Yahweh's gift of sight.

The angel delivered the message to Balaam, using the donkey as an object lesson. Why did Balaam beat the donkey? Because three times the donkey refused to go in the direction Balaam ordered her.

Why did the angel of the Lord oppose Balaam? Because three times Balaam refused to go in the direction the Lord commanded him. Even at that moment if it hadn't been for the donkey, the Lord would have killed Balaam. God was not Balaam's servant. Balaam could not use Yahweh to achieve his own ends.

Balaam was to become Yahweh's servant.

> Then Balaam said to the angel of the Lord, "I have sinned, for I did not know that you stood in the road against me. Now therefore, if it is evil in your sight, I will turn back" (Numbers 22:34).

Balaam's heart must have pounded in his chest. He had barely escaped death. He was quick to confess. But his confession had all the trademarks of someone who had been caught, rather than someone who had been convinced they were wrong.

In 2 Corinthians 7 Paul wrote about two kinds of sorrow—worldly sorrow and godly sorrow. Worldly sorrow is based on having been caught and being in despair. Those who experience worldly sorrow are sorry because of their situation and the consequences of their sin. But those who experience godly sorrow are sorry because they realize they have sinned against a holy God and turned away from grace. They are convinced (convicted) by the Holy Spirit that what they have done is truly wrong, and their hearts are pierced. They are internally motivated to change. Their consequences don't cause a change in direction—what God does in their hearts causes a change in direction.

Balaam confessed that he had sinned, but he followed it with "for I did not know that you stood in the road against me." Balaam believed that he had transgressed because he didn't know better. He acknowledged that he was wrong—not because he'd realized his own heart was at odds with God—but because he saw that an angel was about to kill him. He claimed ignorance, as if to say, "I'm sorry God. I didn't know that this was wrong. If this is wrong, I can go back." Balaam struggled to learn that God rules and God intended to have His way with Balaam's life.

God cared about what was in Balaam's heart. He cared about Balaam's intentions. And he cared about Balaam's motives for obedience. Balaam may not have repented from his heart, as the rest of the story bears out, but he had had a near-death encounter with the angel of the Lord. And though Balaam would not be motivated to obey God out of love or loyalty to him, He was motivated to obey God out of fear.

> And the angel of the Lord said to Balaam, "Go with the men, but speak only the word that I tell you." So Balaam went on with the princes of Balak (Numbers 22:35).

The angel of the Lord reiterated God's command. God's constraint was burned on Balaam's heart with fear. He couldn't say whatever he wanted. He could only say what God commanded.

If only God would burn the same command on our hearts and minds. We must have an ultimate commitment to be constrained by the Holy Spirit and God's Word in order to faithfully speak God's message. We must give our hearts over to God to speak His Word alone.

God loves us so much that He sent Jesus to die on the cross for our sins while we were still sinners. He forgave us. He rescued us. He loved us in our failure and weakness, and He restored us from our sins. We should be motivated by this love and set our hearts on His Word alone.

But if we aren't motivated by that love to live a holy life and minister God's Word alone, the fear of discipline and judgment should motivate us in our immaturity.

God's heart for you and for me is to be a true prophetic people and priests of God. If we set our hearts to obey God's will and constrain our mouths to His Word, we will be that true prophetic people. If we turn our hearts away from God we will fall into the error of Balaam.

We may maintain our reputations as ministers. We may still be able to prophesy accurately. We may be lauded and loved by the people. We may be successful. But we will lose true spiritual sight. Donkeys will have a clearer vision of the spiritual world than we will.

God told Balaam to go, but to "speak only what I tell you." And then to leave. Balaam wasn't supposed to add anything of his own.

Balaam obeyed this command when it came to prophetic blessings over Israel. But before the story ended Balaam tried to circumvent the Lord's command.

---

1. Allen, Ronald B. Numbers (The Expositor's Bible Commentary) (Kindle Location 10000). Zondervan. Kindle Edition.

SIX
BALAAM'S FIRST ORACLE

When Balak heard that Balaam had come, he went out to meet him at the city of Moab, on the border formed by the Arnon, at the extremity of the border. And Balak said to Balaam, "Did I not send to you to call you? Why did you not come to me? Am I not able to honor you?" Balaam said to Balak, "Behold, I have come to you! Have I now any power of my own to speak anything? The word that God puts in my mouth, that must I speak." Then Balaam went with Balak, and they came to Kiriath-huzoth. And Balak sacrificed oxen and sheep, and sent for Balaam and for the princes who were with him.

And in the morning Balak took Balaam and brought him up to Bamoth-baal, and from there he saw a fraction of the people (Numbers 22:36-41).

Balak was so intimidated by the Israelites and so eager to get started, he rushed to the border of Moab to meet Balaam. When he met Balaam, he chided him for not coming sooner and reminded him that he could reward Balaam financially. He was pressuring the prophet.

Pastors and people within the body of Christ place similar pressure on prophetic ministry today. They want the prophets to produce, and they are eager for prophetic messages. They want a prophetic blessing.

People will always be eager to hear God's voice, but sometimes they are not as eager to hear it for themselves as they are to hear it from an intermediary. What's more, many struggle to understand the prophetic gift and ministry and what it requires. Many are excited to have a source of prophecy that they can direct to produce. Many are less excited to have an individual with a gift they can't control.

Balak made an even greater mistake. He persisted in believing that Balaam could curse and bless as he chose. Balaam had encountered the Lord in a way that had taken his speech away from him. He had been scared straight. He was now wholly dependent on God.

> Balaam said to Balak, "Behold, I have come to you! Have I now any power of my own to speak anything? The word that God puts in my mouth, that must I speak" (Numbers 22:38).

This was the fourth time Balaam spoke this phrase, and this time I think it really came from the heart. Balaam meant it.

We may pay lip service to saying what God says, to speaking the words that God puts in our mouth, but we must be vigilant over our hearts and mouths. Balaam proceeded under the threat of losing his life. Speaking only the word of Yahweh was no longer lip service. It was life or death.

The Sacrifices

> Then Balaam went with Balak, and they came to Kiriath-huzoth. And Balak sacrificed oxen and sheep, and sent for Balaam and for the princes who were with him. And in the morning Balak took Balaam and brought him up to Bamoth-baal, and from there he saw a fraction of the people (Numbers 22:39-41).

Balak didn't seem concerned with Balaam's confessed inability to speak apart from the God of Israel's will. Balak, like so many of us, was a practical man. He cared about what would work. He knew that Balaam's curses worked. He also knew that money was an effective motivation.

Balak sacrificed oxen and sheep, perhaps partly in preparation for the ritual curse, but almost assuredly as a feast of honor for Balaam.[1] In the morning, Balak took Balaam to a mountain where he could see part of the people of Israel. In Balak and Balaam's world of magic, heights were important. They were thought to demonstrate advantage both physically and spiritually. It was important to be able to see the enemy to curse them, and the mountains were thought to increase one's proximity to the gods.

The "high places" were points of access for the spiritual realm and plagued Israel as places for idol worship. Some charismatics and proponents of more extreme views on spiritual warfare still seek "high places" where they believe their prayers and their own actions and prophetic words of blessing and cursing will be augmented. This is not the what Jesus taught. The kingdom and authority of Christ is within.[2] Jesus associates with the lowly and demonstrates his power through the humble. The more humbly submitted we are to Jesus, the greater we can be used as a conduit of his authority and power.

> And Balaam said to Balak, "Build for me here seven altars, and prepare for me here seven bulls and seven rams." Balak did as Balaam had said. And Balak and Balaam offered on each altar a bull and a ram (Numbers 23:1-2).

Though Balak was king, Balaam took over. He knew how to access power and clearly had respected experience in reaching the gods and releasing curses.

The sacrifices Balak made should not be confused with the sacrifices Israel was commanded to make. Balaam's sacrifices were used for divination. The death of the animals was meant to attain the favor of the god they sought and the livers and organs of the animals would be used in divination to read and interpret the will of the god.[3] Balaam continued to seek Yahweh in the way that he knew how—through divination and magic.

Balaam's way of seeking God was expensive. It cost a lot to sacrifice so many animals to the gods. It took time, manpower, and preparation. Balak and Balaam were willing to pay the price.

Today we can approach the throne of grace boldly and freely. God requires no sacrifices anymore. Jesus has opened the way with His own blood. We don't have to read God's will in the livers of animals. He has written His law on our hearts. He reveals His will in His Word and by His Spirit.

Yet, though the price has been paid by Christ, do we value our freedom to approach God? Do we invest as much as these pagans did? Are we willing to pay the cost of our time? Are we willing to prepare to meet and hear God? Are we willing to pay the price to our lifestyles and our entertainment? Are we willing to pay the price to give up our own desires and submit to God when He reveals His?

Today you can meet with God. No sacrifice is required.

Seven Sacrifices on Seven Altars

> Balaam tells Balak to build...seven altars and offer seven bulls and seven rams. A Babylonian tablet describes a similar procedure: 'At dawn [cf. 'in the morning', 22: 41], in the presence of Ea, Shamash and Marduk [Babylonian deities], you must set up seven altars, place seven incense burners of cypress and pour out the blood of seven sheep'. 11 Sometimes the ritual was even more elaborate and needed to be repeated eight times. When this had been done the diviner presented himself before the deity and reminded him of the offerings (cf. 23: 4).[4]

Balaam's process parallels what the Babylonian tablet describes. He prepared the seven sacrifices and ordered Balak to stand beside them. Then he went off on his own to meet God.

> And Balaam said to Balak, "Stand beside your burnt offering, and I will go. Perhaps the Lord will come to meet me, and whatever he shows me I will tell you." And he went to a bare height, (Numbers 22:3).

Balaam isolated himself on a mountain to hear God. While I mentioned earlier that Balaam saw heights as more spiritual and spiritually effective than he should have, going to a mountain alone was also the habit of Moses and Jesus in the New Testament.

Mountain heights are hard to get to. The effort is worth it if it results in a place where you can meet with God alone away from distractions and surrounded by His creation. This isn't always possible, but if, like Balaam, I was seeking the ideal place to hear God's voice, a mountain seems like an excellent choice.

> ...and God met Balaam. And Balaam said to him, "I have arranged the seven altars and I have offered on each altar a bull and a ram" (Numbers 23:4).

When God met Balaam, Balaam again followed the prescription the Babylonian tablet outlined. He presented himself to the deity, Yahweh, and reminded him of the sacrifice he had made. This reveals Balaam's mindset. He was still approaching Yahweh the way he would any other deity. He viewed Yahweh as someone to be appeased and cajoled. He viewed Him as someone who could be bribed and who could change his mind.

This process was about persuasion. But there is something to learn from Balaam's process. We too should seek to meet the Lord alone. And when we find Him, we should present *ourselves* as living sacrifices.[5] We should give him our bodies as instruments of righteousness. We should dedicate our hands and feet to His service. We should dedicate our mouths to His Word. And we should remind ourselves of His great sacrifice for us. We can approach Him with confidence, not because we have made a ritual sacrifice to please Him, but because Jesus Christ's eternal sacrifice stands before Him and we are now His righteousness, forgiven and cleansed by perfect blood. We approach as Sons of God. Not as hired diviners.

> And the Lord put a word in Balaam's mouth and said, "Return to Balak, and thus you shall speak." And he returned to him, and behold, he and all the princes of Moab were standing beside his burnt offering (Numbers 23:5-6).

Although Balaam approached God in the wrong way, God still met with Balaam and He put His word—a prophetic message—in Balaam's mouth. God treated Balaam as His own servant. God still uses unclean vessels.

When he returned, all the princes of Moab with all their influence, their money, and their honor were standing there. They were hoping for a Word from God that would destroy their enemies. He would have to displease them all.

Whether we realize it or not, most of us experience pressure from others regarding how we speak and serve in ministry. People want to be encouraged. They want to be blessed. They want to be told that God loves them and is happy with them and with everything they are doing.

They want specific, detailed words that will help them plan their life. They want their dreams and plans confirmed. They want their expectations met. While some people believe that prophetic people are just naturally more resilient to these pressures, much of what I read in the Bible reveals men and women who struggled with their gifting and calling.

Part of developing character in prophetic ministry is learning to say what God says in the face of opposition and expectations. For all of Balaam's flaws, he faced the pressure and "took up his discourse."

> And Balaam took up his discourse and said,
> "From Aram Balak has brought me,
> the king of Moab from the eastern mountains:
> 'Come, curse Jacob for me,
> and come, denounce Israel!'" (Numbers 23:7).

Balaam started out his first prophetic word with an introduction of the occasion and purpose of the prophecy. This prophetic message wasn't coming to someone who was open to any Word from the Lord. Balak specifically wanted to curse Israel. Balaam had been hired for a very specific purpose.

Balaam was clear up front. He couldn't do what Balak hired him to do. Balak and the Moabites would be disappointed. From their perspective this would be Balaam's greatest failure. From God's perspective this would be His greatest accomplishment.

> How can I curse whom God has not cursed?
> How can I denounce whom the Lord has not
>   denounced?

> For from the top of the crags I see him,
> from the hills I behold him;
> behold, a people dwelling alone,
> and not counting itself among the nations!
> (Numbers 23:8-9).

Balaam could not curse these people because God had not cursed Israel. The Israelites were different. When Balaam saw Israel through God's eyes he didn't see a nation like others. He saw a unique people who were holy. They were set apart to God and by God. They stood alone among the nations.

> Who can count the dust of Jacob
> or number the fourth part of Israel?
> Let me die the death of the upright,
> and let my end be like his!" (Numbers 23:10).

Balaam could not count the people. At the end of his first word he began to intimate the future of the people. Their future would be prosperous. They had multiplied through the earth. While God promised Abraham descendants like the stars in the sky, Balaam saw them as the dust on the ground. Balaam's prophecy ended on a personal note as his own desire and personality came into the prophetic word. He wished his own life would end in the prosperity and glory He saw in Israel's future.

This first prophetic word confirmed that Balaam could only say what God said. His words—which were not seen simply as statements of truth, but as active blessings and curses—would go out into the spiritual realm and cause effective change. This first word only began to reveal the character of Israel. God saw them as holy. God saw their future as they became an innumerable people. God had a salvation and end for them in glory. Balaam saw this and his own personality came into the message as he expressed a yearning and a desire for God's blessing.

All of us have a specific personality. We are distinct from every other human being and that shows in the way we talk, in the way we think, in what words we choose, and in how we minister. Even when we minister prophetically, our culture, language, and personality come through. This was true for the biblical prophets; it was true for the authors of the New Testament who were inspired to write Scripture; it was true for Balaam; and it is true for us today. God works with us, and He works with our personality. He doesn't make us robots or completely overwhelm who He has created us. He wants our distinct voice.

There are times when our personalities can hurt our ministry. Our loud, confrontational style may not perfectly represent the Lord. Our meek and quiet delivery may not instill the awe or courage God wants to convey. But it's okay for our personality to come through. We shouldn't seek to wipe our personality out of prophetic ministry, any more than we should attempt to prophesy in Aramaic or Greek. But we shouldn't allow our personality to overwhelm our ministry either.

The strongest prophetic words are the words that contain the most content from Christ's heart. Balaam's first prophetic word is powerful and stands for eternity in Scripture. But I would argue that far fewer people have found this word as powerful, touching, or applicable as Christ's words to the Seven Churches in Revelation chapters two and three. Those words are pure messages from Christ. The Apostle John simply wrote down what he heard without interpretation. He was hearing from Jesus face to face, and he reported what he heard with accuracy. This resulted in a powerful word that has continued to apply across cultures and to many personalities for two thousand years. Balaam's word is very much part of a time and place.

We must understand that it is not wrong for our personalities to come through during prophetic ministry. This is inevitable. But we should seek the purest word we can from Christ. When Jesus speaks to us clearly and unveiled, we should speak clearly and without filters, interpretation, or personality. If we can report what Christ says verbatim, we are truly prophesying as Christ would—a true gift from the Holy Spirit.

By some standards Balaam's first oracle would be considered a weak prophecy. It contains no specific information. It contains a general blessing about Israel's current holiness and future multiplication. And, it includes a personal expression from the prophet. But this is only the beginning. As Balaam was faithful with the first prophetic word. God entrusted Him with more revelation.

But first he had to face Balak's fury.

Facing the First Disappointment

> And Balak said to Balaam, "What have you done to me? I took you to curse my enemies, and behold, you have done nothing but bless them." And he answered and said, "Must I not take care to speak what the Lord puts in my mouth?" (Numbers 23:11-12).

I wonder how Balaam must have felt facing Balak's anger. Most people do not take criticism well. It's often even harder when people criticize your service. This is something all ministers deal with. Jesus was perfect, and he faced murderous opposition.

Many people care less about whether a prophetic word is accurate than they care about what the word means for them and their lives. Many people are not sincere enough to desire correction if they are wrong. Narrow is the gate that leads to life and few there are that find it.[6]

How we respond to criticism in the New Covenant is important. We have to acknowledge that we could have been wrong. Balaam didn't do this, but Balaam is also something of a special case. He was having divine encounters over every prophetic word. Similarly, I wouldn't have expected the Apostle John to say, "Well, I could have been wrong about Revelation."

There are occasions when a revelation is so strong, and our inner confidence is so grounded by the experience that we don't have to back down. Our testimony is like this. The Lord spoke to us in some way, we believed, and we don't have to question or look back. The gospel is true and real in our lives.

But we all see in part and prophesy in part (1 Corinthians 13:9). We are all prone to error. We can all "miss it." Especially in spontaneous settings where prophecy is expected.

Prophetic ministers no longer operate as lone gifts like they did in the Old Testament, but as members of the body of Christ and subject to the community discernment of the body of Christ. Others get to judge prophecy. And this means we must be willing to confess that we could be wrong.

I was recently listening to a prophetic minister who has been faithfully prophesying for over forty years. He is one the most credible prophetic ministries I know. And he said when he was faced with criticism he had to acknowledge, "I might have missed it [....] My most common prayer is, 'God don't let me screw this up.'"

We have to have the same humility and commitment to correction as we desire the rest of the body of Christ to have. Only one minister never made mistakes: Jesus Christ. All other ministers make mistakes. Every single one. Apostles make mistakes. Evangelists make mistakes. Shepherds make mistakes. Teachers make mistakes (what Bible teacher do you know who is right in every detail of their doctrine?). Prophets make mistakes.

In the New Testament we don't stone prophets. We judge prophecy. We don't kill people for their mistakes, we kill the effectiveness of their mistaken word.

For this part of his ministry, Balaam did well. He knew what he heard from God. Balak had no relationship with Yahweh, and he certainly didn't have the Holy Spirit or the ability to judge prophecy. He simply wanted what he wanted.

Balaam confidently responded with the same words I hope I can say, and I hope that each of you can say:

Must I not take care to speak what the Lord puts in my mouth?

---

1. Cole, Dennis R. Numbers: An Exegetical and Theological Exposition of Holy Scripture: 3 (The New American Commentary) (Kindle Location 11225). B&H Publishing Group. Kindle Edition.
2. Luke 17:21
3. Allen, Ronald B. Numbers (The Expositor's Bible Commentary) (Kindle Locations 10033). Zondervan. Kindle Edition.
4. Wenham, Gordon J. Numbers (Tyndale Old Testament Commentaries) (pp. 193-194). InterVarsity Press. Kindle Edition.
5. Romans 12:1
6. Matthew 7:14

SEVEN

BALAAM'S SECOND ORACLE

And Balak said to him, "Please come with me to another place, from which you may see them. You shall see only a fraction of them and shall not see them all. Then curse them for me from there." (Numbers 23:13)

Cursing Israel was Balak's only hope for victory. He was not one to give up easily. Balak decided to apply some of his own spiritual knowledge. He wanted the diviner to try again, but this time from a different vantage point.

Numbers were important to Balak, and he thought numbers were important to the gods, too. Perhaps, he thought, if they were not confronted with the whole number of the Israelites, but only a fraction; they would be more inclined to curse Israel rather than bless them.

> And he took him to the field of Zophim, to the top of Pisgah, and built seven altars and offered a bull and a ram on each altar. Balaam said to Balak, "Stand here beside your burnt offering, while I meet the Lord over there" (Numbers 23:14-15).

Balak followed the same pattern of offering seven bulls and rams on seven altars. Balaam gave Balak the same instructions and went to meet Yahweh again. He was just as confident as he was before that God would meet him, but it seems like with each encounter Balaam learned more of Yahweh's character and desires. Regardless of this growing knowledge, Balaam approached Yahweh through divination again.

> And the Lord met Balaam and put a word in his mouth and said, "Return to Balak, and thus shall you speak" (Numbers 23:16).

Yahweh met with Balaam again, and the Scriptures repeat the same summary as before. This time Balaam did not present his sacrifices as a trade or even as leverage. Balaam was learning that Yahweh was not affected by his sorcery or divination.

> And he came to him, and behold, he was standing beside his burnt offering, and the princes of Moab with him. And Balak said to him, "What has the Lord spoken?"

> And Balaam took up his discourse and said,
> "Rise, Balak, and hear;
> give ear to me, O son of Zippor…" (Numbers 23:17-18).

Balaam didn't give a corporate prophetic word. This time the word God gave him was personal. God had a specific message for Balak. This is just one example of many personal prophetic words in the Old and New Testament. God wanted Balak to understand something. He wanted to reveal part of His character, and what He revealed to Balak remains as one of the most encouraging promises we have about the nature of God.

> "…God is not man, that he should lie,
> or a son of man, that he should change his mind.
> Has he said, and will he not do it?
> Or has he spoken, and will he not fulfill it?" (Numbers 23:19).

Yahweh is not like human beings. He does not lie. He is completely and thoroughly honest. He is true. Every word He says is true. He fulfills every single promise to us. He follows through on every single thing He says He will do. God is ultimately, finally, and thoroughly trustworthy. He is faithful from the beginning to the very end. God does not lie.

God is not capricious. He does not go back on His promises or His plans. God is not fickle. God is not arbitrary. He cannot be manipulated or persuaded with sacrifices. God cannot be bought. God does not change His allegiances. God's love doesn't wax or wane.

We can impact God through relationship with Him and participate in His rule and reign. We can see our prayers answered. We can intercede like Moses and interact with God in His plans, but His character and His faithfulness remain unchanging. He is honest and faithful, steady and reliable.

Through the prophetic, Balaam was realizing and revealing to Balak that Yahweh was not like the gods they knew. The gods they knew were like human beings. They had human failings and human passions. The gods and their favor were constantly shifting and changing. They were unpredictable and untrustworthy.

Yahweh is completely different. He is resolute and unchanging. In a capricious and unpredictable world, Yahweh is a constant. His character, mood, and purpose would not change. No amount of divination could make him change. No amount of magic. He is unbound and unmoved by ritual, sorcery, or fleshly endeavor.

This was a stunning revelation to Balaam and his worldview. This was truly mysterious. They had never encountered a god like Yahweh.

> Behold, I received a command to bless:

> he has blessed, and I cannot revoke it (Numbers 23:20).

Balaam's perspective came into the prophetic word again. He spoke to Balak from his own experience and revelation of Yahweh. Yahweh had ordered Him to bless Israel, and Yahweh's mind could not be changed. Balaam was under the duress and control of God now. He must bless, and he could not take it back.

While Balaam was bound by power, we are bound by the love and fear of the Lord. May we have the same concrete stance on God's Word and will. May we be given over to God's will.

> He has not beheld misfortune in Jacob,
> nor has he seen trouble in Israel.
> The Lord their God is with them,
> and the shout of a king is among them (Numbers 23:21).

Balaam turned His eyes to the subject of God's love and gave a prophetic word that illuminates God's perspective. We read the Book of Numbers, and we see evil everywhere. We see trouble. We see misfortune. We remember sin after sin. We remember rebellion after rebellion. This is a sinful people. This is a tragic people— a people wandering and lost in the wilderness—barred from what God had promised them.

Yet God did not keep their sin in mind.

He did not see them as trouble or in trouble. He saw them with the eyes of love and promise. He saw their position as His children. He declared His love for them and their good standing with Him. These were the people of His covenant. They could not be cursed.

They were in a relationship with God, and God was with them. In an incredible insight Balaam declared God King in the midst of Israel. This is the first mention of God as King in the entire Bible. This image points forward to the coming King of the Messiah, the promise of God's kingdom and God's rule and reign in His kingdom of love. It is because of this rule and reign that God was able to use Balaam in this way and Balaam, pagan as he was, could still declare Yahweh's rule. Yahweh was with Israel as a conquering king. He would spread His reign over this land and through this people.

> God brings them out of Egypt
> and is for them like the horns of the wild ox.
> For there is no enchantment against Jacob,
> no divination against Israel;
> now it shall be said of Jacob and Israel,
> 'What has God wrought!' (Numbers 23:22-23).

Yahweh had conquered divination and witchcraft before. Moses' showdown with Pharoah's magicians had wrecked economic and physical destruction on the nation of Egypt. The miracles God did in Egypt remain a testament to God's ability and power.

When God speaks his Word through us, it is tailored to our personality and culture. The culture of the kingdom shines through, but He speaks from what is familiar to the prophet and the audience. The horns of the wild ox (or aurochs) was a symbol of strength to this culture, a symbol they understood.[1]

No enchantment would work against Jacob. No sorcery can succeed against God's people. God protects them, and magic, divination, curses, and all forms of witchcraft can't undo God's choice or impact God's plan for His people. Balak's plan was doomed to failure.

Not only will cursing and sorcery not work against Israel, but Yahweh cannot be swayed with divination or enchantment. This was an open rebuke to Balaam and Balak.

Because no enchantment or divination could be used against Israel, what became of Israel could only be attributed to Yahweh Himself. The Israelites were not a nation of powerful diviners who had held their deity in sway. They had not manipulated Yahweh or bound Him to their success. Yahweh Himself worked in the nation for His own pleasure and power.

"What has God wrought!" God Himself was in control of their lives, in the crossing of the Red Sea, in the manna during the journey, in the crushing of rebellion, and in the wilderness. God alone was the source of their success and their victory.

Israel's victory was not only not of their own strength, it was not even their own idea. This was God's plan and will from the days of Abraham. God initiated the plan. God was the one who accomplished it.

Balaam not only saw his own failure, but the futility of Balak's mission. The Moabites would fail. Israel would destroy them.

> "Behold, a people! As a lioness it rises up
> and as a lion it lifts itself;
> it does not lie down until it has devoured the prey
> and drunk the blood of the slain" (Numbers 23:24).

Balaam prophesied Israel's victory in graphic terms. Israel would not leave a Moabite alive. The lion would not scatter its enemies. It would not cause them to flee. It would kill them all and drink their blood. Israel would consume the life of her enemies.

Can you imagine standing before a crowd of people and prophesying God's opposition to them and His complete destruction of their plans?

Balaam rendered a powerful blessing on Israel and a powerful curse on Moab and its people. Balaam did the opposite of what Balak asked him to do. He prophesied directly in the face of the pressure placed on him.

Balaam, who has a universal reputation as a false prophet and false teacher, did not give in to the pressure. He was compelled by the Lord and was faithful to the Lord's message in spite of the expense paid by his hosts and in spite of the fee and money he was promised.

> And Balak said to Balaam, "Do not curse them at all, and do not bless them at all." But Balaam answered Balak, "Did I not tell you, 'All that the Lord says, that I must do?'" (Numbers 23:25-26).

Balak was horrified and understandably so. Balaam had spelled out his doom. He was beside himself. Hiring Balaam had been worse than doing nothing. He pleaded with Balaam to stop. He never expected this. Balak was a practical man, and he had practical expectations.

Balaam, however, was bound by another's will.

In what must have started sounding like a song on repeat, Balaam reminded Balak, "Did I not tell you, 'All that the Lord says, that I must do?'"

Balaam was not only saying that he couldn't have said anything different. He was also saying that he could not have been silent. He could not have quenched or refused to release this prophetic word.

If only I was under such constraint. I have quenched the Spirit again and again. I have felt the burn to say something inside me and turned away from it again and again. Like Jeremiah I determined not to speak.[2]

Balaam, as an example of a false prophet, should instruct those who consider themselves true servants of God. His commitment to say only what God had told him rebukes those who prophesy out of their independent minds and spirits. His commitment to meet with Yahweh to find out what to say rebukes those who prophesy lightly and without preparation or intimacy with God. His refusal to stay silent, but to deliver the word that God gave him rebukes every person who has denied the Lord the opportunity to speak through them.

Balaam was not motivated properly. He was trying to manipulate God, and he cared little for God's plan. But as a professional diviner or "prophet-for-hire" he had an integrity in his communication that I wish all of God's people had.

This commitment to speak God's Word may have come from a mixture of motives. It may have been a matter of personal or professional pride. It may have been fear. Or maybe he simply did not believe there was a different way to minister. He was compelled.

God's people are free. Prophets are not puppets, and God is not a puppet master. We have choices to make in how we minister and how we speak. We have a choice whether to open our mouths or stay silent. We have a choice about whether we will choose to meet with God, or whether we will minister in our own strength and from our own resources.

May we truly offer our bodies as living sacrifices. May we offer our mouths to God's service everyday of our lives and commit our hearts to him, so that when the pressure is on and when we stand in immense spiritual conflict we can say like Balaam, "All that the Lord says, that I must do."

---

1. Allen, Ronald B. Numbers (The Expositor's Bible Commentary) (Kindle Locations 10273). Zondervan. Kindle Edition.
2. Jeremiah 20:9

EIGHT
BALAAM'S THIRD ORACLE

And Balak said to Balaam, "Come now, I will take you to another place. Perhaps it will please God that you may curse them for me from there." So Balak took Balaam to the top of Peor, which overlooks the desert. And Balaam said to Balak, "Build for me here seven altars and prepare for me here seven bulls and seven rams." And Balak did as Balaam had said, and offered a bull and a ram on each altar (Numbers 23:27-30).

Balak still didn't believe or understand what Balaam was telling him. He wanted to keep trying to curse Israel, and he thought once again that a change in geography might change the outcome of Balaam's words. Balak didn't mention that this change in geography would change the view of Israel's numbers. In fact, the text doesn't mention that this new location would give Balaam a view of Israel at all, which may indicate that Balak chose it for a different reason.

Whether we want to admit it or not, many believers have the same superstitions about place that Balak had. They hold their church sanctuary in reverence and see it as a holy place. There is nothing wrong with setting a place apart for God. But God and God's power are not bound to a place. Nor is the movement of the Holy Spirit. The Holy Spirit can move just as much in a small group in a home or in an encounter in the workplace or on the street as He can in a church building. Almost every believer would say *amen* to this. But do we act like it?

Baal Peor

Balak had more in mind than just a high mountain or a more advantageous view of the enemy. He took Balak to the "top of Peor." This place is also known as Baal Peor, a place which would become infamous later in Scripture.[1] This was the center of Baal worship.

Baal was a false god who would have an enormous impact on Israel's history. Baal is mentioned about 90 times in the Bible. Of all the false gods that appealed to Israel in their idolatry, Baal was the most popular. But Israel had not met Baal when Balaam first entered Israel's story.

The reason Balak chose Baal Peor is not clearly stated, but the location suggests several things. First, Balak could have reasoned that this was the domain of a different god, so Yahweh would be weakened. This was a common view, and one that consistently tempted Israel. They were enticed by the new gods who had been worshipped in the unfamiliar places they settled. They saw Yahweh as the old god who had been present to take them out of Egypt, but had no power in this new geography. If they wanted to prosper in this new land, they thought they had to worship the gods of their current geography.

Another reason Balak may have chosen Baal Peor may have been that he was requesting that Balaam get a prophetic word or curse from Baal instead of from Yahweh.[2] Regardless of what Balak intended, Balaam had begun to learn from his experiences with Yahweh, and he did not seek Baal or seek to manipulate Yahweh. In giving up those methods he found the purest prophecy of his life.

Balaam's Third Oracle

> When Balaam saw that it pleased the Lord to bless Israel, he did not go, as at other times, to look for omens, but set his face toward the wilderness. And Balaam lifted up his eyes and saw Israel camping tribe by tribe. And the Spirit of God came upon him, (Numbers 24:1-2).

Although he still ordered Balak to make sacrifices, Balaam didn't try divination. He didn't seek omens or attempt sorcery.

He knew none of these things would work. Yahweh was in control of what was happening. Balaam did not even go to meet Yahweh again. He knew what Yahweh's answer would be, and he knew that Yahweh was ready to bless Israel. He didn't need to ask again.

Instead of going through a process to acquire revelation and a supernatural message, Balaam looked out at Israel. As he did, the Spirit of God came upon him, empowering him to prophesy. A pagan diviner was anointed and empowered by the Holy Spirit of God to declare His word over His people.

The previous prophetic words were the result of Balaam's prophetic abilities obscured by practices of divination and attempts to manipulate God. Now, empowered by the Holy Spirit, Balaam's words took on a new weight and authority. Balaam saw a greater revelation than he had before. He saw into the future and into God's plan, not only for Israel, but for the entire world.

> and he took up his discourse and said,
> "The oracle of Balaam the son of Beor,
> the oracle of the man whose eye is opened,
> the oracle of him who hears the words of God,
> who sees the vision of the Almighty,
> falling down with his eyes uncovered:
> (Numbers 24:3-4).

Balaam "saw" that it pleased the Lord to bless Israel, and because of that he began to see in the Spirit clearly. God's will was no longer veiled or varied in Balaam's mind. It was absolute. Balaam's spiritual eyes were "uncovered." Balaam the seer was blind to the angel on the road, but as he aligned himself with the will of God, he saw clearly.

Balaam saw Yahweh as "the almighty"—the most powerful God. He saw God's truth and God's plan regarding Israel. He received genuine revelation in a vision—without divination or human contamination. And he fell down in submission. Seeing in the Spirit can mean seeing angels, receiving visions from God or revelation about spiritual activity. But even more importantly in means having God's perspective and understanding His plan.

This is an important truth for each of us who wishes to see in the Spirit and have a prophetic ministry. Gifting, skill, and training may be able to produce some results that impress people, but only true submission to the will and Word of the Lord allows someone to truly see in the Spirit. The least gifted believer in submission to Christ will live a far greater prophetic life and have a far greater prophetic ministry than the most gifted prophet whose abilities stay on the periphery of God's will and purpose. The success of this world—fame, acclaim, and finances—may go to the merely gifted and skilled, but eternity will applaud the faithful.

Balaam went from being a diviner who was deceived and blind in the Spirit to being an effective instrument in God's hand. And, as the story later reveals, his heart hadn't even changed. He had simply decided to submit and obey Yahweh in the moment. When he gave in to God's desire he became equipped for God's purpose. As we surrender our hearts to Christ, the Spirit will equip us for His work, which includes the divine and prophetic leading. We can go beyond Balaam from a moment of faithfulness to a lifetime of faithful service.

> Although Balaam himself is to be regarded as morally and spiritually degenerate, his reception of the message of Yahweh is as authentic as that of any prophet of the Old Testament.[3]

Some interpret Numbers 24:3-4 to mean that Balaam went into an ecstatic trance (losing consciousness) when God's Spirit came upon him—that God's Spirit took away his will at this point and used him like a puppet. This is speculative, but not impossible. There are clearly times when God uses people against their will. Saul was on a trip to kill David when he came into the presence of prophets and began to ecstatically prophesy (1 Samuel 19:18-24). God has a way of using even homicidal enemies as vessels and mouthpieces.[4]

Whether God put Balaam into an ecstatic trance or not, Paul clearly wrote that the spirit of the prophets are subject to the control of the prophets (1 Corinthians 14:32). We can and must control ourselves for the glory of God. We should seek to minister faithfully out of our good relationship with God as our master. He should not need to forcefully control us or overwhelm us. These things can happen, but they are clearly not the norm in the New Testament and not necessarily desirable. We should surrender ourselves to God and seek to serve Him to our utmost in the capacities He has given us.

While I do believe that God initiates emotionally or spiritually ecstatic experiences within His church—the day of Pentecost seems to be one—it is also clear that "decently and in order" is the norm and that these ecstatic experiences did not result in a loss of consciousness for the believers.[5] This was also the norm for the Hebrew prophets, who prophesied from an experience with God with clarity and personality as well as conscious understanding.

Ecstasy was the norm for Ancient Near Eastern religions. Their prophetic ecstasies featured a loss of personal control and consciousness, resulting in a prophetic message they did not comprehend or intend. A different spirit or being possessed them during this time. This was almost certainly the work of demons.[6]

Those in the New Covenant are one with God and our spirits are in union with the Holy Spirit.[7] He works with us. While His presence may be overwhelming, He doesn't kick us out of our minds to use us. God only does that to His enemies.

Regardless of whether Balaam prophesied out of an ecstatic experience, his words were nothing short of incredible. He clearly saw Israel's future and God's love and attitude toward His people. He prophesied from the Father's heart.

> How lovely are your tents, O Jacob,
> your encampments, O Israel!
> Like palm groves that stretch afar,
> like gardens beside a river,
> like aloes that the Lord has planted,
> like cedar trees beside the waters
> (Numbers 24:5-6).

Balaam saw the tents of Israel and saw the beauty of the order that God had created. He saw the tabernacle with God's presence at the center surrounded by the priests and Levites. He may have even seen the cloud of Yahweh's glory residing above the camp ready to lead the people.

Balaam saw this order, and what he saw transformed before his eyes. He saw future cities, homes, and buildings. He saw a lush garden. A natural paradise created by God for His people.

What will you see when you look at God's people?

> Water shall flow from his buckets,
> and his seed shall be in many waters;
> his king shall be higher than Agag,
> and his kingdom shall be exalted (Numbers 24:7).

Israel would be blessed with water and seed, king and kingdom. Water and seed point to material prosperity and multiplication. God would make Israel's land fertile and Israel fertile and virile as a people. But this physical prosperity points to a greater spiritual prosperity. Israel's King would be greater than all kings. His Kingdom would be exalted. Balaam could not have known the great Kingdom of Christ which has come and is coming now on the earth, spreading in the hearts and through the lives of those who believe.

> God brings him out of Egypt
> and is for him like the horns of the wild ox;
> he shall eat up the nations, his adversaries,
> and shall break their bones in pieces
> and pierce them through with his arrows (Numbers 24:8).

Balaam recited the song of praise surrounding Israel's salvation from Egypt. God was bringing them out. And He is the one who is powerful like a wild ox. This reference back to the second oracle deepens the thought. It is Israel's God who has the power. He is the one who fights for them. He is the one who eats up the nations and breaks them. He is a mighty warrior.

> "He crouched, he lay down like a lion
> and like a lioness; who will rouse him up?
> Blessed are those who bless you,
> and cursed are those who curse you" (Numbers 24:9).

Here Balaam prophetically echoes God's promise to Abraham:

> "I will make you into a great nation,
> and I will bless you;
> I will make your name great,
> and you will be a blessing,
> I will bless those who bless you,
> and whoever curses you I will curse;
> and all peoples on earth
> will be blessed through you" (Genesis 12:2-3).

This promise flew in the face of everything Balak intended, and Balaam pronounced a curse on Balak and all of Israel's enemies even as he blessed them.

The Consequences

And Balak's anger was kindled against Balaam, and he struck his hands together. And Balak said to Balaam, "I called you to curse my enemies, and behold, you have blessed them these three times. Therefore now flee to your own place. I said, 'I will certainly honor you,' but the Lord has held you back from honor" (Numbers 24:10-11).

Balak was furious. Balaam had not only stubbornly refused to do what Balak had asked him to do, he had done the opposite.

This is the third time anger is mentioned in Balaam's story. First Yahweh's anger burned against Balaam because of Balaam's attempts to use sorcery and divination to manipulate God. Then Balaam's anger burned against his donkey as his plans to go with the princes of Moab were interrupted for the third time. Balak's anger burned against Balaam as Balak's plans were frustrated by Yahweh for the third time. While God's anger was provoked first, God's powerful work frustrated the enemies of Israel and the intentions of every man who opposed the will of God. God's anger led to God frustrating Balaam's plans and making Balaam angry. Balaam came under submission to God, provoking Balak. Anger had come full circle back on God's enemies.

Balak told Balaam to get out. He sent Balaam packing. He was clear. Balaam would receive no honorarium. Balak would not pay or honor him.

Balak had not hired him to speak the Word of the Lord. He had hired Balaam to help accomplish his own plans. He did not care about the plans of God.

Many people are like Balak today. Many believers are like Balak. Many pastors and leaders are like Balak. They value prophetic ministry. They love power. They believe prophetic ministry can accomplish great things in their lives and in their ministries.

But they don't really want a word from God.

They want God and the prophet to confirm their own plans and their own ministries. They want a blessing on their intentions and dreams and a curse on everything that opposes them. They don't want to hear anything different. They want to purchase prophetic assurance. They want an outside ministry to come and approve of their plans and their dreams.

And they are willing to pay for it.

Like Balaam's divination business, ministry that confirms the plans of church leaders can be highly lucrative. You can receive honor. You can be at the top of people's lists of respected and known prophets.

But you may not be serving the Lord at all. You may just be reading people's desires, allaying people's fears, and confirming people's dreams. And you would be doing it for money and honor. You would be prostituting the prophetic.

Many people are so focused on success and self-promotion they lose their hearts. And with their hearts, the Word of the Lord. They may still be able to operate in prophetic gifts. They may still impress. But they have gone astray. Even if God uses them to deliver his divine Word, their ministry, like Balaam's would be shipwreck.

Similarly there are numerous Balaks in the world, as well. Nearly every single person who pursues the Lord's work the Lord's way will be confronted by someone who wants to use and control them.

You may have to stand before Balak and explain why you didn't minister the way he wanted you to. You may have to give up your reputation and honor. You may have to give up financial reward.

Balaam, for all his flaws, had some backbone. He had told Balak's messengers and Balak himself that he was bound to speak what the Lord told him.

> And Balaam said to Balak, "Did I not tell your messengers whom you sent to me, 'If Balak should give me his house full of silver and gold, I would not be able to go beyond the word of the Lord, to do either good or bad of my own will. What the Lord speaks, that will I speak?' (Numbers 24:12-13).

Balaam wanted money. That was clear. But he sincerely believed that he could not go back on what the Lord said.

For Balak, Balaam's ministry was over. He would not hire Balaam again. Balaam would receive no reward. He was sending Balaam on the two-week journey home empty handed. Balaam wouldn't even receive compensation for his travel.

Balak's fury overcame his fear of Israel. There was nothing he could do. He would have to try to face Israel on his own.

But Balaam wasn't done. He still had a message to deliver. And from his own mouth he had said that he couldn't hold back anything that God had told him to say. Again, I am convicted at how often I have kept words to myself. Balaam knew he had to speak—not only about Israel's future, but about the future of Balak and the Moabites.

---

1. Numbers 25:18, 31:16, Joshua 22:17
2. Allen, Ronald B. Numbers (The Expositor's Bible Commentary) (Kindle Locations 10346). Zondervan. Kindle Edition.
3. Allen, Ronald Barclay. The Theology of the Balaam Oracles: A Pagan Diviner and the Word of God (Unpublished doctoral dissertation) p. 295. Dallas Theological Seminary, Dallas.
4. Cole, Dennis R. Numbers: An Exegetical and Theological Exposition of Holy Scripture: 3 (The New American Commentary) (Kindle Locations 11906-11911). B&H Publishing Group. Kindle Edition.
5. 1 Corinthians 14:40
6. Heschel, Abraham Joshua. The Prophets, II. P.133-134. Prince Press.
7. 1 Corinthians 6:17

NINE
BALAAM'S FINAL WORDS

"And now, behold, I am going to my people. Come, I will let you know what this people will do to your people in the latter days" (Numbers 24:14).

Balaam openly promised to tell the future. He would tell Balak what would happen "in the latter days." Balaam was seeing events thousands of years beyond his own time. He saw beyond the first coming of Christ to the second.

Balaam's fourth oracle or prophetic word didn't require any sacrifices or rituals. He didn't go aside to meet with God again, and he had finally given up all divination, sorcery, and attempts to manipulate God and His message.

Instead, the prophetic word that God had seeded into Balaam's heart in his previous encounters with Yahweh came bursting forth. This word didn't come by Balak or Balaam's initiative. This was what God wanted said and when God wanted it said.

Though God in His power and rule uses unholy vessels, I doubt that Balaam could have given this prophetic word until now. Its richness and power were available to him only after he had heard and seen the Lord, Balaam's will had been broken, and he had faithfully delivered God's initial messages.

Each of Balaam's words escalated in depth and prophetic insight. The fourth and final message revealed God's future plan with the power of the gospel. This message was referenced by Hebrew prophets and stands as one of the first Messianic prophecies in the Bible.[1]

> And he took up his discourse and said,
> "The oracle of Balaam the son of Beor,
> the oracle of the man whose eye is opened,
> the oracle of him who hears the words of God,
> and knows the knowledge of the Most High,
> who sees the vision of the Almighty,
> falling down with his eyes uncovered:"
> (Numbers 24:15-16).

Balaam introduced the fourth oracle in the same way he introduced the third, but this time he added "knows the knowledge of the Most High." Balaam had not only seen and heard God, he had received supernatural knowledge of God's plan. God had shared His mind with Balaam.

No matter your past, God can still speak to you and through you. Sometimes I am amazed that God speaks to me at all. I'm amazed when God speaks through some friends and acquaintances I know. I'm amazed when people I'm helping through addiction receive revelations from God, as well. From the very beginning God has spoken into darkness.

We are no different than Abraham. He used his power over Hagar to try to produce an heir and then cast her out. God shared His plan with Abraham and today Abraham's descendants are as the stars in the sky because of God's blessing and promise. We are no different than Jacob, who lied and deceived his way into wealth and blessing. He met with God, and God blessed him. We are no different than Jonah or David or Jesus's disciples. God has always revealed Himself to broken and twisted humanity. He reveals Himself to you.

The question is what will we do with the revelation God has given us? Abraham believed God and that faith acquired righteousness. Jacob placed his trust in God. David repented of his sins and saw the future covenant God promised. The disciples were empowered by the Holy Spirit and gave their lives changing the world for Christ.

Balaam's story winds down a different way, but like all of these other flawed men and women, he too could have received the promise. The fact that he wanted the promise[2] but didn't receive it and even turned away from it for momentary gain makes his gospel prophecy even more poignant.

> "I see him, but not now;
> I behold him, but not near:
> a star shall come out of Jacob,
> and a scepter shall rise out of Israel;
> it shall crush the forehead of Moab
> and break down all the sons of Sheth" (Numbers 24:17).

Balaam saw God. He saw Jesus. Not in his time period or ours, but in the future of God's reign when Christ will inaugurate God's kingdom. He saw a ruler arising out of Israel, who will crush the enemies of God's people.[3]

He saw a star coming out of Jacob, a prophecy fulfilled at Christ's birth. The birth of the incarnate King was declared by the heavens by the star that appeared over Bethlehem (Matthew 2:1-10).[4] He saw a scepter rising out of Israel. The royal scepter or staff was a clear representation of rule, authority, and power in the culture. The Israelites of the time would be reminded of Jacob's blessing of Judah in Genesis 49:9-10—a promise that Judah's royal lineage would go on forever. Readers of the New Testament can look forward to Christ's rule with a "rod of Iron" on the last day (Revelation 2:27).

Even more incredible than these Messianic predictions coming from an enemy of Israel is the stunning statement that the Almighty God who Balaam saw in verses 15 and 16 *is* the coming Messiah in verse 17. Balaam prophesied the mystery of the incarnation long before it occurred.[5]

God's power and the power of the inspiration of the Holy Spirit is so great that He can overwhelm every obstacle to His message. No background in sorcery, no past immorality, no current personality can drown out the Word of God when God decides to speak. When God chooses to do something, He achieves his purpose.

It is true that Balaam had some virtues and took some actions that thrust him into God's plan. He believed that he could meet Yahweh. He sought Yahweh diligently. He received discipline until he was truly determined to prophesy only what God said. If we want to be used by God in this way, we should attempt to learn to seek God and hold those convictions. But we can never earn the ability to meet with God or hear His voice.

Today we live in the New Covenant, and that was earned by Christ on the cross. Now each of us can stand in full assurance of faith before God's throne. Not because God wants to use us against his enemies, as He did Balaam. But because God truly wants us to know and experience Him.

> "Edom shall be dispossessed;
> Seir also, his enemies, shall be dispossessed.
> Israel is doing valiantly.
> And one from Jacob shall exercise dominion

and destroy the survivors of cities!" (Numbers 24:18-19).

This ruler who comes out of Israel and Jacob will rule over the earth. He will rule in justice. Balaam didn't see the coming of the humble Savior, but the coming of Christ the King in Revelation 19 who comes to judge in truth and justice. He saw the end before the beginning. And like many prophetic messages, this one would be misunderstood.

> Then he looked on Amalek and took up his discourse and said,
> "Amalek was the first among the nations,
> but its end is utter destruction."
> And he looked on the Kenite, and took up his discourse and said,
> "Enduring is your dwelling place,
> and your nest is set in the rock.
> Nevertheless, Kain shall be burned
> when Asshur takes you away captive."
> And he took up his discourse and said,
> "Alas, who shall live when God does this?
> But ships shall come from Kittim
> and shall afflict Asshur and Eber;
> and he too shall come to utter destruction."
>
> Then Balaam rose and went back to his place. And Balak also went his way (Numbers 24:20-25).

Balaam prophesied the destruction of all of Israel's enemies and the nations he names remain types or symbols of the enemies of God's.[6] These words may seem anticlimactic to us, who see the glory of the coming Savior and King. But in context, this was a stunning final blow to Balak's plans. Balaam had cursed Balak and his people. He had concluded his prophetic words with a deathblow to Moab and all of Israel's enemies. God had a final revenge on all the attempts to curse Israel and on all the attempts of pagan manipulation. They would ultimately be destroyed along with every force the devil attempted to use to destroy God's people.

Balaam had been given knowledge of God's will and plan. With that knowledge came a choice. He could align himself with Yahweh's will and begin to pursue the glorious end that God's people receive. He could exit Israel's story and continue his life as an ancient Near Eastern diviner. Or he could continue to oppose God's plan and make himself the target of the message God had given him and perish as God's enemy.

---

1. Allen, Ronald Barclay. The Theology of the Balaam Oracles: A Pagan Diviner and the Word of God (Unpublished doctoral dissertation) p. 310. Dallas Theological Seminary, Dallas.
2. Who can count the dust of Jacob
    or number the fourth part of Israel?
    Let me die the death of the upright,
    and let my end be like his!" Numbers 23:10
3. These verses are hotly debated among scholars, but the Jewish commentators of the Qumran clearly saw these prophecies as

Messianic, and the early church fathers identified these verses as pointing to Christ. While some scholars argue that these verses may refer to David rather than to Jesus, even David points to Jesus as a type and shadow of Christ. The mainstream evangelical scholars I have found the most helpful agree that these words point to Christ's incarnation and second coming. I have included an exegetical paper I wrote on Balaam's fourth oracle as an appendix in this book. I encourage you to read the appendix and the following footnotes for more information.

4. The glory of this King is portrayed using two metaphors, the "star" and the "scepter". Isaiah used the star imagery in the context of royalty in describing the coming fall of the king of Babylon (Isa 14:12–13), and in the New Testament Jesus Christ is referred to as the royal "Root and Offspring of David, the Bright Morning Star" (Rev 22:16). His birth as the incarnate King was declared by the heavens in the appearance of a star over Bethlehem (Matt 2:1–10). The Qumran sectarians interpreted this passage as having Messianic import, as did other Jewish sources of the period between the mid-second century B.C. and the first century A.D.623

    Cole, Dennis R. Numbers: An Exegetical and Theological Exposition of Holy Scripture: 3 (The New American Commentary) (Kindle Locations 12102-12108). B&H Publishing Group. Kindle Edition.

5. See Cole above and Allen, Ronald B. Numbers (The Expositor's Bible Commentary) (Kindle Locations 10560-10568). Zondervan. Kindle Edition.

6. Allen, Ronald B. Numbers (The Expositor's Bible Commentary) (Kindle Locations 10665-10666). Zondervan. Kindle Edition.

TEN

BALAAM'S FINAL ACTIONS

Then Balaam rose and went back to his place. And Balak also went his way (Numbers 24:25).

The final verse of Numbers chapter 24 shows Balaam and Balak parting ways. They were both defeated. Balaam found himself unable to bless Israel and instead gave three blessings and a prophecy about the coming Messiah and His rule and the destruction of all of Israel's enemies. He left without the pay or honor he came for. Balak left with a curse of doom hovering over himself and his people.

God had manipulated the manipulators and overpowered the diviners, the gods, and the enemies of Israel.

The Next Chapter

Numbers 25 opens without any mention of Balaam, and it seems like Balaam's story is over. Balaam prophesied accurately. He did so at the loss of pay and prestige. And he did so under intense pressure.

If this is the end of his story, why does the Bible call him a false prophet?

Even though Numbers 25 doesn't contain Balaam's name, it is a continuation of Balaam's story. Balaam's shadow looms over Numbers 25-31. While Balaam stayed out of the spotlight, what he did off-stage changed Israel's history forever.

The Bible tells Balaam's story out of chronological order. Balaam doesn't get mentioned again until Numbers 31. For the sake of this book and clarity I'm going to recreate the story in chronological order.

Balaam's Key Decision

Balaam left knowing that he had failed. He failed to turn Yahweh against Israel. And he knew that he would never be able to. But he had been able to acquire some valuable information about Yahweh and Israel.

Yahweh was Israel's strength. He was their protector. He was their guardian, their victory, and their assurance of success. He was their invincibility in battle.

Balaam knew that Yahweh was loyal to His people. He would not change His mind. Yahweh would never betray or turn away from His people.

But would Israel turn away from Yahweh?

If he couldn't find a way to get Yahweh to turn away from Israel, could he get Israel to turn away from Yahweh? Could Balaam find a way to turn the Israelites away from their source of strength and power? Balaam made a new plan.

He knew enough of Yahweh to know that Yahweh was holy and valued holiness. Yahweh was One and demanded that the Israelites worship Him alone. *Perhaps if the Israelites deserted Yahweh in favor of another god, Balaam and Balak could find a way to defeat them. Perhaps Yahweh Himself would destroy them.*

Balaam came to Balak with a new plan and a new way to earn his honorarium. In the book of Revelation Jesus explained what Balaam did in His letter to Pergamum.

> Nevertheless, I have a few things against you: There are some among you who hold to the teaching of Balaam, who taught Balak to entice the Israelites to sin so that they ate food sacrificed to idols and committed sexual immorality (Revelation 2:14).

Balaam went to Balak and schemed to get Israel to worship idols. They would not conquer Israel through military strength. They would conquer Israel through seduction.

Balak and Balaam decided to send women to seduce the Israelite men. These women would willingly tempt the Israelites with sex and pleasure. They would entice them with orgies and a sexual "freedom" Yahweh would never give them. They would promise to make the Israelite men's sexual fantasies come true. And in the process, they would introduce the source of this sexual freedom and pleasure: their god —Baal.

Moses later said of these women:

> They were the ones who followed Balaam's advice and enticed the Israelites to be unfaithful to the Lord in the Peor incident, (Numbers 31:16a).

Only in the aftermath of Israel's actions does the Bible reveal Balaam and Balak's plans. In God's eyes they were only secondary actors. They had no power over Israel. Israel had a choice to obey God and live a holy life, fleeing from sexual immorality. God held Balaam and Balak responsible for putting a stumbling block in front of Israel. But God also held Israel responsible for their own sins. In God's eyes, what happened in Numbers 25 was between Him and Israel more than it was between Israel and Balaam.

BALAAM'S GOD

The transition from Numbers 24 to Numbers 25 is jarring. The narrative goes from an incredible story of God's blessing, covenant, and enduring love of Israel to the depths of unfaithfulness by God's people. This was more than rebelling against Moses. This was far more dangerous than complaining about food and water in the wilderness. This idolatry would have consequences for generations.

Moab Seduces Israel

> While Israel was staying in Shittim, the men began to indulge in sexual immorality with Moabite women, who invited them to the sacrifices to their gods. The people ate the sacrificial meal and bowed down before these gods. So Israel yoked themselves to the Baal of Peor. And the Lord's anger burned against them (Numbers 25:1-3).

Balaam's plan worked. The Moabite women succeeded in seducing the men of Israel. They followed these women and joined themselves to them in sex. Their bodies united in the presence of all, and as each of these men had intercourse with Moabite women during a ritual sacrifice to Baal they pledged their allegiance to a new god.[1]

> Baal was the great Canaanite fertility god, whose worship Israel always found very alluring (e.g. Judg. 2: 13; 1Kg 18; 2Kg 17: 16; Jer. 2: 8, etc.). By participating in this cult Israel had yoked or coupled himself to Baal of Peor (3). In so doing

143

> they flagrantly repudiated the essential heart of the covenant, total and exclusive allegiance to the LORD,[2]

They bowed before Baal. They worshipped him. And in their sexual ecstasy they gave their lives and souls under the dominion of a demon.

> Do you not know that he who unites himself with a prostitute is one with her in body? For it is said, "The two will become one flesh" (1 Corinthians 7:16).

Sex is powerful. The chemicals released in the brain during sex are more powerful than heroin and cocaine and have a bonding effect. Sex has been an integral part of sorcery, magic, and idolatry since ancient times. Many still believe and practice sex magic as the ecstasy brought on at the climax of sex is thought to have the power to release the intention of a spell, blessing, or curse. Similarly, taboo or perverse sex is thought by some to have power in the spiritual world. Oracles and cult prostitutes were famous for their prophetic abilities which were tied directly to sex with the subjects of their prophecy. While some may dismiss these practices as superstitious, Israel's history and the rest of the Bible teach that sex is indeed powerful and deeply spiritual.

Sexual temptation is one of the enemy's strongest tools, and he still uses it to lead astray. In today's culture sex is not so strongly tied to religion. People have sex freely without considering anything spiritual happening or thinking that they are joining themselves spiritually to another person. They certainly don't think that they are submitting to a demon's desires. But this is where illicit sex led the Israelites.

The Israelites could not conceive of a sexuality that was not tied to spirituality and worship.

The person in front of the computer for hours obsessed with watching pornography submits and subjects himself to demonic activity also. It may not be as explicit as the Israelites. But many find themselves bound in ways that go beyond a simple, natural explanation. They find that they have ceded a part of their will and part of their life over to a different power.

God's justice was quick and absolute. And this time Moses did not intercede.

> The Lord said to Moses, "Take all the leaders of these people, kill them and expose them in broad daylight before the Lord, so that the Lord's fierce anger may turn away from Israel" (Numbers 25:4).

God commanded Moses to kill the leaders of the people and to publicly display their dead bodies. Their deaths were meant to stand in for the death of the people. This was the mercy of God on display. God would allow the leaders to stand in for the people and take the punishment for them.[3]

> So Moses said to Israel's judges, "Each of you must put to death those of your people who have yoked themselves to the Baal of Peor" (Numbers 25:5).

Moses, whether in agreement with the judges or of his own decision, decided instead to let the people die for their own sins. The leaders would not take the place of the offenders. Many more people would die, but Israel would still be purged of sin. Moses chose the greater judgment.

> Then an Israelite man brought into the camp a Midianite woman right before the eyes of Moses and the whole assembly of Israel while they were weeping at the entrance to the Tent of Meeting (Numbers 25:6).

As Moses sought a solution and to execute the justice of God, the unthinkable happened. A son of one of Israel's leaders named Zimri[4] brought a Midianite woman from Baal Peor and the site of Baal worship into the camp of Israel. This Midianite woman's name was Cozbi[5] and the cultural context and the fact that she was a Midianite in the midst of Moabites indicate that she was most likely a noble and a priestess of Baal.[6] This couple was not just in the throes of ecstasy and drunkenness. There was purpose and intention behind their actions.

The Hebrew reveals much more about this passage than the English.[7] According to scholars, Zimri brought Cozbi into the camp of Israel and began to have sex with her in the entrance of the Tent of Meeting. He went from having sex and worshipping Baal in the camp of Baal to bringing one of the priestess to the altar of Israel and performing an act that would bind his people to Baal as a whole.

This was meant to be an act of power. He intended to transform the altar, the tent, and the people of Israel by dedicating them to Baal through sexual magic.

They wanted to transform the place of worship into a place of orgies and sexual fantasy. They wanted a different religion. They wanted a god who would give license to their lust. They did not only want to pledge themselves to Baal as individuals —they wanted the whole of Israel to belong to Baal.

They may have been losing themselves in sexual ecstasy. They may have been caught up in the pleasure of the moment. But a greater force was influencing their behavior.

Satan had an intentional plan and used pleasure to guide them into the place where he could take control of Israel or wipe them out. Even if he failed, he could get God's punishment to fall on them. He would stop the coming of the Savior through the human race and the people of Israel. He would stop God from keeping His promise to His people.

A Different Kind of Intercession

When Phinehas son of Eleazar, the son of Aaron, the priest, saw this, he left the assembly, took a spear in his hand and followed the Israelite into the tent. He drove the spear into both of them, right through the Israelite man and into the woman's stomach. Then the plague against the Israelites was stopped; but those who died in the plague numbered 24,000. (Numbers 25:7-9)

"The whole assembly of Israel" saw Zimri and Cozbi fornicating in the Tent of Meeting. So much was happening so quickly. Sin had overtaken the camp. Moses had commanded the leaders to kill every person who had fornicated with the Moabites. Now one of the children of the leaders and a Midianite priestess were defiling the Tent of Meeting. This was shocking and horrifying.

How should they respond? The people froze. One man took action.

Phinehas was not paralyzed with fear or indecision. He was from a family of priests and understood God's law. This was punishable by death. He had heard Moses' orders. He took a spear and thrust it through both the man and the woman as they were in the act. As he did so, the plague of God's judgment halted.

The text does not say when the plague began, but the verses come one after another as action piled into action. A crescendo of horror was building. The Israelites were committing sexual immorality with foreign women. They were worshipping foreign gods. Moses commanded the leaders to kill the sinning Israelites. An Israelite and a Midianite priestess were going to commit sexual idolatry at the Tent of Meeting, defiling it as an act of Baal. A plague was spreading through the camp.

The frenzy froze as Phinehas drove his spear through the couple.

In the aftermath, almost 10% of the Israelites had died in the plague. All of this had happened suddenly. If Phinehas had not had the courage to take action, the Israelites could have been destroyed.

> The Lord said to Moses, "Phinehas son of Eleazar, the son of Aaron, the priest, has turned my anger away from the Israelites. Since he was as zealous for my honor among them as I am, I did not put an end to them in my zeal. Therefore tell him I am making my covenant of peace with him. He and his descendants will have a covenant of a lasting priesthood, because he was zealous for the honor of his God and made atonement for the Israelites" (Numbers 25:10-13).

God commended Phinehas "as zealous for my honor among them as I am."

Zealous for His Honor

God is looking for people who are zealous for his honor. That's an odd phrase today. We don't think about honor as much as those in the eastern part of the world, but honor played a major role in the motivations of the forefathers of the faith. And because of that, it was an important part of how God communicated to them. We may struggle with the idea of being honored today, but we can all recognize that God is worthy of honor.

God is worthy of renown and glory. He is worthy of a reputation for holiness that spans the earth. He is worthy of praise and worship. He is worthy of obedience.

All of these things are connected to God's honor. When God's people obey and worship Him, God is honored and held in good honor. When his people, who are called by his name, disobey him, God Himself is dishonored.

We don't respect parents whose children mistreat them. We think poorly of parents whose children misbehave. What about God's children?

God is dishonored by the sin and idolatry of His people. We understand this, but many ministers are far more motivated by compassion for God's people and by mercy than they are by God's honor. This is the heart of a shepherd, and it is appropriate for us to love God's people. We should have compassion on the sinner and the lost sheep. We should mourn with those who mourn. And we should mourn over sin as God does. But we should also value God's honor and reputation. Paul did. He warned the churches that God's name would be blasphemed because of their evil behavior.[8]

It's the heart of the prophet and the priest to have a grave concern over sin and idolatry—to have a zeal and an anger that motivates holiness. How dare we betray the Creator of the universe? How dare we betray the Master who bought us? How dare we betray the one who loved us and purchased us with His own blood? How can we dishonor God before the eyes of the world with our sexual immorality, our lies, our greed? How can we dishonor God before the principalities and powers that watch in the heavenly realms?

Phinehas had a zeal for the name and glory of God. He had a zeal for holiness and devotion. He had a burning desire for God to be honored and obeyed. This qualified him for leadership. Many people receive leadership because of their giftings: their ability to speak, their administrative gifts, their good people skills—even their anointing. Phinehas was promised leadership because he had a deep passion for people to obey and worship God.

Do you have a burning desire to see God worshipped? Do you have a burning desire to see God loved and obeyed?

Phinehas was a man of action. The whole assembly saw what was happening at the Tent of Meeting. They understood the horror and perversion that was about to occur. But they did not act.

Phinehas, in his zeal for God, took a spear and cut sin out of the community. Many of us do not have the courage, the strength, or the willingness to act against the sin we see in the church. Many people bemoan the statistics that the majority of believers not only view internet pornography but are addicted to it. Many bemoan greed and pride in the church. They see sexual immorality poisoning marriages. But they do not act.

What will you do about the attack of the devil in your church? Will you talk about it with others? Or will you do something? Will you start a purity group in your church? Will you intercede for the youth in your church by name? Will you start a counseling ministry? Will you start mentoring someone you know is struggling with sin? Will you offer to be an accountability partner with someone? A prayer partner? What action can you take?

But before you take the spear in your hand, look at your own heart. Do you have a speck in your eye? Or a log? What is your status before the Lord? Are you living a holy life? Have you done whatever it takes to be free from sin in your own life? Are there actions you need to take to live and be holy in your own walk and talk with God? Have you been open and transparent with others about your own struggles?

Zeal mixed with hypocrisy is pure poison. I can't think of how often God has been dishonored because those who preached holiness did not live it. Every scandal subjects God and the church to ridicule—and it keeps the ridiculers from entering the Kingdom.

Some of us need to take courage and zeal, pick up a spear, and confront idolatry and disobedience with love and strength. Many more of us need to leave the camp of Moab ourselves. We need to flee from immorality. We need to break the bond we have made with sexual immorality, or greed, or spiritual manipulation and divination or whatever sin has hooked our hearts.

A time of judgment is coming for all of us. Be sure that your sin will find you out. Turn today and be found among the faithful. It is never too late to turn from sin and begin to minister the holiness of God for His glory and honor.

> The name of the Israelite who was killed with the Midianite woman was Zimri son of Salu, the leader of a Simeonite family. And the name of the Midianite woman who was put to death was Cozbi daughter of Zur, a tribal chief of a Midianite family.
>
> The Lord said to Moses, "Treat the Midianites as enemies and kill them. They treated you as enemies when they deceived you in the Peor incident involving their sister Cozbi, the daughter of a Midianite leader, the woman who was killed when the plague came as a result of that incident" (Numbers 25:14-17).

God's true leaders wage war on sin. The false prophets and teachers secretly sneak sin into the church. The next chapter presents the Bible's teaching on how to avoid the Balaams of today.

---

1. Allen, Ronald B. Numbers (The Expositor's Bible Commentary) (Kindle Location 10775). Zondervan. Kindle Edition.
2. Wenham, Gordon J. Numbers (Tyndale Old Testament Commentaries) (p. 208). InterVarsity Press. Kindle Edition.
3. Zondervan. 2016. NIV Cultural Backgrounds Study Bible: New International Version. (p. 274). Zondervan.
4. Numbers 25:14
5. Ibid.
6. Allen, Ronald B. Numbers (The Expositor's Bible Commentary) (Kindle Location 10899). Zondervan. Kindle Edition.
7. Ibid. Locations 10921-10899
8. Romans 2:24

ELEVEN
BALAAM'S END

The Lord said to Moses, "Take vengeance on the Midianites for the Israelites. After that, you will be gathered to your people" (Numbers 31:1-2).

God commanded Moses to "take vengeance" against the Midianites for how they had deceived the people of Israel and seduced them into serving Baal. Moses sent the Israelites to wage war on Midian with Phinehas as one of the leaders. God gave them a great victory, and they killed every single Midianite man:

Among their victims were Evi, Rekem, Zur, Hur and Reba— the five kings of Midian. **They also killed Balaam son of Beor with the sword** (Numbers 31:8).

Even though Balaam had spoken God's Word accurately and faithfully, he perished in God's judgment. God took vengeance on him because he'd led the Israelites astray. He was a false teacher—not because he prophesied falsely or inaccurately, but because he enticed the people to follow false gods.

> If a prophet, or one who foretells by dreams, appears among you and announces to you a sign or wonder, and if the sign or wonder spoken of takes place, and the prophet says, "Let us follow other gods" (gods you have not known) "and let us worship them," you must not listen to the words of that prophet or dreamer. The Lord your God is testing you to find out whether you love him with all your heart and with all your soul. It is the Lord your God you must follow, and him you must revere. Keep his commands and obey him; serve him and hold fast to him (Deuteronomy 13:1-4).

God specifically warned His people in this passage that sometimes these prophets would have power. Sometimes they would be able to tell the future. Sometimes they would be able to perform miracles. These people demonstrated supernatural power. Whether or not their abilities were real was not the issue that required discernment. These leaders with their real power and false messages would test whether the people would love God with all their heart and would be faithful to Him.

There are some in the charismatic church today who love miracles and the supernatural more than they love God or the truth. They will follow whoever can promise them the greatest experience. Whoever can perform the biggest signs or wonders, or whoever can perform the most unusual miracles will get their loyalty and their attention regardless of character, message, or the fruit of the ministry.

It is appropriate to love God's miraculous works and to desire to see God move in miraculous ways. I long to see the Holy Spirit move people's hearts, and I have seen many gifts of the Spirit and many signs and wonders. But I am in love with the Lord Himself. I will only follow Him. No demonstration of power, no matter how great, impressive, or emotional will convince me to stop believing the gospel or stop following Jesus as my Master.

I remember sitting in a "minister's meeting" where a man was giving personal prophecies to the crowd. He had a group of other men with him who were walking up and down the aisles and through the seated crowd as he ministered. They would come and go, whispering in the man's ear.

It was unclear what these assistants were doing, but the fact that everyone at the conference had name tags made their activity seem suspect. His assistants could have easily been Googling the names of the people in the crowd.

His prophetic ministry consisted of detailed words of knowledge, naming the counties people lived in, the church they served at, and various other details about their lives. This was followed by rather general prophetic words. Several times it was verbatim, "And God says He is going to give your church revival."

There was nothing wrong with this ministry per se. I felt that the way he was ministering encouraged skepticism. It was easy to doubt the source of his knowledge when his assistants were whispering to him so often. I was unsettled but tried to persuade myself to be open and full of faith.

At one point in the service he said that he was entering a phase of ministry called a "prophetic smorgasbord." He called a man out of the service and told him, "God has told me that he is going to give you whatever you ask for. So what would you ask for right now?" The man was shocked and baffled. He stammered in surprise before finally saying, "I just want more of the Lord." The minister rolled his eyes and said, "But what do you want God to bless you with?" The man said, "I want more of the anointing." The minister rolled his eyes again and told the man, "Sit down. Sit down. I was going to tell you that God would give you whatever you wanted, but you didn't have the boldness to ask for it [....] You should have asked for money." He went on to teach more about money, but I had heard enough at that point.

I got up and walked out of the service. This minister had told a man that his desire for God was wrong and that he should have pursued money instead. There were several questionable things about this man's ministry. I had strong convictions about his misuse of Scripture, but I had been willing to continue to believe the best and continue to discern. When he redirected this man and the crowd to pursue money and demeaned this man's sincere desire for God and the Holy Spirit it went too far.

This man was leading people to another god.

The Warning of the Law

The Old Testament Law does not apply to us today, nor do its punishments, but they do stand as a warning of what God hates.

The punishment for leading God's people to false gods was death.[1]

In Deuteronomy 18 God prescribed laws about those who practiced divination and those who prophesied and claimed to be prophets. These were Old Covenant Laws and are not binding for us today, but I believe they are important because they describe God's heart. These laws are only the starting point for revelation about prophets and prophecy, but they are an important starting point that God revealed to His people.

> When you enter the land the Lord your God is giving you, do not learn to imitate the detestable ways of the nations there (Deuteronomy 18:9).

God makes it clear that He does not want His people to imitate the way of life that the other nations practiced. He wanted His people to be separate. But these laws were more than that. These laws were distinctly about universal holiness. They weren't just about a culture or uniqueness or being set apart for God. God called these practices "detestable." These were things that God judged in every nation, not only the nation of Israel.

> Let no one be found among you who sacrifices their son or daughter in the fire, who practices divination or sorcery, interprets omens, engages in witchcraft, or casts spells, or who is a medium or spiritist or who consults the dead. Anyone who does these things is detestable to the Lord; because of these same detestable practices the Lord your God will drive out those nations before you. You must be blameless before the Lord your God (Deuteronomy 18:10-13).

God hates child sacrifice. He also hates divination and sorcery, interpreting omens, witchcraft, casting spells, consulting the dead or necromancy as well as being a medium or spiritist. God forbids these things not only for Israel but says that he will judge the rest of the nations for doing them as well. These practices may seem obviously wrong to you, but they are more prominent than you might think.

Any initiation of reading of symbols or random phenomena in order to "prophesy" or discern the future *outside of direct rela-*

tionship and communication with God may in fact be divination. Mediums, spiritists, and necromancers may seem out of the middle ages, but they exist today. Most of the people reading this will have seen a movie or a TV episode that depicted a séance or a ghost or spirit communicating through a human being.

A friend once recommended a Christian counseling book on finding freedom from addiction to me. One of the techniques described in the book was summoning dead parents or relatives in your imagination and having conversations with them about past wounds. One of the patients who used this technique summoned his dead missionary father and ended up "discovering" that his father was in fact to blame for the wounds that resulted in his pornography addiction.

I believe that speaking to dead relatives in your imagination to cause a spiritual or emotional cure is in fact necromancy. Do not do it. At best you open yourself to deception and hearing from lying sources.

The same is true for those who seek to get information from demons. I know a missionary who formed a major part of his theology about demons and the spiritual world by interviewing demons who were currently possessing people. This too, is wrong. We should not be seeking spiritual information from demons. And we certainly should not let them inform our worldview. Demons lie. We are commanded to cast them out, not to interview them and use their victims as mediums.

I am not saying that the people who do these things are liars or frauds. I believe that they are genuinely encountering and interacting with spiritual phenomena. I am not saying that they are not believers. They are living in a dangerous practice. These practices are sin and are forbidden by God. If you are involved in any of these practices, please repent! God is more than enough for us and the source of all the information we need. He loves us and holds our future in his hand. There is no information that you can get through divination or demons that you need to have and can't get from God.

> His divine power has granted to us all things that pertain to life and godliness, through the knowledge of him who called us to his own glory and excellence, (2 Peter 1:3).

The Promised Prophet

These were sins that resulted in the fall of nations and the judgment of God. The body of Christ should have no part of them. God draws a powerful contrast between Jesus the Prophet and the sorcerers of the day.

> The nations you will dispossess listen to those who practice sorcery or divination. But as for you, the Lord your God has not permitted you to do so.
>
> The Lord your God will raise up for you a prophet like me from among you, from your fellow Israelites. You must listen to him. For this is what you asked of the Lord your God at

Horeb on the day of the assembly when you said, "Let us not hear the voice of the Lord our God nor see this great fire anymore, or we will die" (Deuteronomy 18:14-16).

At Horeb the Israelites felt fear in the presence of God. Even though He wanted a direct relationship with them they trembled and felt fear in His presence. They cried out and asked God not to speak with them directly. They wanted Moses to speak to them for God. They made a deal with God. They would listen to Moses, but they would not interact with God for themselves.[2]

This desire is still prevalent among some of God's people. Some do not want direct access to God. They fear his voice. They want an intermediary. Sometimes they choose their leader. Sometimes they choose to simply make themselves deaf to God's voice and the leading of the Spirit. Sometimes they want to only listen to the Bible and disregard anything else. They will take God's general leading, but they want to be able to choose specifically for themselves how to apply the Bible rather than let the Holy Spirit and God's voice apply it to their lives.

Still others fear God in an unhealthy way. They do not want to submit to Him. They do not trust Him to really love them. They do not trust His leadership. They would rather fulfill their own desires than His. They don't want to hear God for themselves.

But this is never what God desired. From that time at Horeb, He had a plan to commune with His people by dealing with sin on the cross and sending Jesus Christ as the High Priest.

> The Lord said to me: "What they say is good. I will raise up for them a prophet like you from among their fellow Israelites, and I will put my words in his mouth. He will tell them everything I command him. I myself will call to account anyone who does not listen to my words that the prophet speaks in my name (Deuteronomy 18:17-19).

Peter confirms in Acts 3:19-23 that this prophet is Jesus Christ Himself—our loving Savior. The book of Hebrews says that while God spoke in many ways in the past and in the Old Covenant, today He always speaks through His Son.

> In the past God spoke to our ancestors through the prophets at many times and in various ways, but in these last days he has spoken to us by his Son, whom he appointed heir of all things, and through whom also he made the universe (Hebrews 1:1-2).

Today God speaks through Jesus and all supernatural knowledge and all prophetic revelation must come through relationship with Jesus Christ. Any other source of supernatural wisdom or knowledge about the past, present, or future is forbidden and presents a danger to the believer. Any prophet or anyone speaking from revelation who attributes their revelation to another source or acquires their revelation outside of direct relationship with Jesus Christ is to be held suspect. Any leader advocating a different source of revelation or encouraging believers to trust or follow any idol or source of power must be considered a false prophet.

The Consequences

> But a prophet who presumes to speak in my name anything I have not commanded, or a prophet who speaks in the name of other gods, is to be put to death."
>
> You may say to yourselves, "How can we know when a message has not been spoken by the Lord?" If what a prophet proclaims in the name of the Lord does not take place or come true, that is a message the Lord has not spoken. That prophet has spoken presumptuously, so do not be alarmed (Deuteronomy 18:20-22).

There were two kinds of prophets that God ordered the Israelites to purge from their community. The first was the wrong or inaccurate prophet. This was a prophet who spoke in the name of Yahweh something that God did not command. This prophet spoke presumptuously and was not to be feared or respected. Because the Holy Spirit was not given to all believers at this time, God used only a handful of prophets to speak to the community. The community did not have the gift of the Spirit or the ability to discern God's voice as a whole.

They were dependent upon the prophets. Because of this, prophecy had immense power and required great vigilance. There was no tolerance for mistakes. The prophet who got it wrong was to be killed.

Today, God does not speak through a lone prophet; He speaks through a prophetic community and the community has the responsibility of testing and judging prophecy, not killing prophets. God speaks much more frequently through all believers and with greater grace as we each learn to hear God for ourselves, the greatly gifted prophet and the brand-new believer. The discernment of the community and the gift of the Holy Spirit upon the church keeps us safe even though people make mistakes.

The second kind of prophet that God ordered Israel to purge from the community was the prophet who prophesied from a different source. The prophet who prophesied in the name of Baal, or in the name of Money, or in the name of some New Age force. Any prophet who operated from a different source of revelation, gave a different god glory, or led the people to worship or desire different gods was to be killed. Even if his prophecies were accurate.

By choosing to tempt the Israelites with Baal worship, Balaam chose this second category. Balaam pursued other gods as the source of his revelations. He was a pragmatist. He sought whichever god he needed to please and use to accomplish the results he wanted. He was utilitarian. Religion and spirituality was about whatever would bless him the most.

When he encountered Yahweh, everything changed. Here was a God who could not be manipulated. Here was a God who was not susceptible to divination or sorcery. This God was the most powerful God—the Creator.

This God was not like people. Yahweh was not capricious. He did not lie. He was a God of honor, who fulfilled His word.

Balaam almost lost his life to Yahweh. He nearly died in the encounter with the angel on the road. Balaam knew that obeying Yahweh was the only way to escape his encounter with this God alive. And Yahweh became the source of Balaam's inspiration and revelation. Balaam's methods and prophetic powers greatly changed. He saw the future in new ways and even saw God's greatest plan for the world: Jesus Christ the Messiah.

What could have led him astray? How could he have gone from a place of such power and prophetic revelation and fear of the Lord to being a false prophet?

---

1. Deuteronomy 13:5-11
2. Exodus 19:16-20:21

TWELVE
BALAAM'S WAY

Simon's heart beat with a fresh rhythm of joy. He had thought that he had known all the power the spiritual world had to offer, but he had found new life in the message that God had sent His Messiah to the Jews and that this Messiah had been crucified on the cross for the sins of Samaritans as well. God had raised Him from the dead and given Him rule over God's kingdom.

Simon had been awed not only by this new message, but by the power that accompanied it. The man named Phillip had healed many paralyzed and lame people in the name of this Messiah, and he had cast out the spiritual powers that bound many. Simon had thought these demons powerful, but they shrieked in fear and agony as Philip had commanded them to leave on the authority of this Jesus.

Simon knew spiritual power. He had amazed all of Samaria with his power, and he had not been afraid to boast that he was the Great Power of God. He had built his reputation and his following over many years. But he had never known power like the kind that came with the message of this new Messiah Jesus.

He truly believed, and when Phillip told him to give up his sorcery and be immersed in water, he agreed. He traded his power for loyalty to this new Messiah. His heart was convinced by the power of God, and he followed Phillip everywhere trying to learn the secrets of this power and this kingdom.

Then Philip's leaders, Peter and John came. And they demonstrated the same power Phillip had. In fact, when they laid their hands on people, they were overcome by God's power. The Holy Spirit touched these people.

Phillip had shown that God's power was for everyone, and that this power was in the name and authority of Jesus, not in the holiness or works of the people. But Peter and John seemed to be operating in a different gift.

Simon saw the opportunity to distinguish himself. He wanted this power.

> When Simon saw that the Spirit was given at the laying on of the apostles' hands, he offered them money and said, "Give

me also this ability so that everyone on whom I lay my hands may receive the Holy Spirit" (Acts 8:18-19).

The story of Simon the Sorcerer in Acts 8, which I have retold here, shows a man who was like Balaam in many ways. He was acquainted with the spiritual world and spiritual power. He had a great reputation and following. And he'd had a genuine encounter with God—one that went beyond Balaam's because he'd met Yahweh through the Gospel of Jesus Christ.

Though there are debates as to whether Simon was a true believer, the Bible states that Simon believed and was baptized. We would say that he made a "decision for Christ." But there were areas of Simon's heart that still needed to be evangelized. He longed for power and for spiritual gifts, not so he could bless the body of Christ, but so he could distinguish himself.

You may remember Peter's response to Simon, but take a moment and imagine this situation. How would you respond to Simon if you were Peter? Would you assure Simon that he didn't have to pay, that God gave everything according to His grace and by faith? Would you caution Simon that God was the one who gave gifts? Would you explain that Simon already had this power and didn't need to pay for it? Theologians dispute the meaning of this passage regarding the Holy Spirit and Simon's salvation, but Peter's response goes beyond those theological considerations and cuts to the heart. It is one of the scariest personal prophecies in the New Testament:

Peter answered: "May your money perish with you, because you thought you could buy the gift of God with money! You have no part or share in this ministry, because your heart is not right before God. Repent of this wickedness and pray to the Lord in the hope that he may forgive you for having such a thought in your heart. For I see that you are full of bitterness and captive to sin."

Then Simon answered, "Pray to the Lord for me so that nothing you have said may happen to me" (Acts 8:20-24).

Peter saw Simon's heart, and it was full of evil desire. Simon had believed the gospel. He had seen miracles. He had been baptized in water. But he still wanted power. The desire to manipulate spiritual power, the desire to have control, the desire to be above and better than others, still held his heart.

Peter firmly told him that God would not give him this ministry. He ordered him to repent and receive forgiveness for his evil thoughts and motivation. Simon responded humbly and requested prayer.

The Bible doesn't tell us what happened to Simon after this. Eusebius, the early church's first historian, recorded that Simon the Sorcerer eventually turned away from the faith and started his own cult. He went back to his own ways, becoming a false teacher and a false prophet.[1] If this is true, Simon was following a pattern set much earlier by another sorcerer, who had genuinely tasted the goodness of God.

Balaam's Heart

Balaam stayed loyal to his idols and false gods despite all his encounters with Yahweh. This wasn't because he viewed those gods as more powerful. He clearly experienced that Yahweh was different and more powerful than they were. He did it solely because these gods offered him what he wanted in the moment. They satisfied his lust for money and pleasure.

I can't help but be reminded of how the crowds responded to Jesus' ministry. He performed many miracles. He healed the sick. He multiplied food. He raised the dead. And still people did not believe.

Even those who did believe only followed him because they wanted to see him multiply food again. "But Jesus would not entrust himself to them, for he knew all people." (John 2:24). Jesus answered, "Very truly I tell you, you are looking for me, not because you saw the signs I performed but because you ate the loaves and had your fill" (John 6:26).

The shallow selfishness that Jesus identified in the hearts of the crowd is the same selfishness that leads people away from God today. The lust for pleasure, power, pride, and prosperity pulls at the heart. Passionate disciples of Jesus who do not remain vigilant to guard their hearts can find themselves set on these same temporal desires.

Divination didn't lead Balaam astray. Desire for money did. Many of us look at the false teachers of the day and feel great confidence that we are not like them. But we must acknowledge that only God's grace and submission to Him can keep us from succumbing to the same temptations they did. We are human, too. And we are subject to the same human desires that ensnare false teachers.

False Teachers Among You

In 2 Peter the apostle explains the presence of false teachers in the past, including Balaam, and explains their presence in the future.

> But false prophets also arose among the people, just as there will be false teachers among you, who will secretly bring in destructive heresies, even denying the Master who bought them, bringing upon themselves swift destruction. And many will follow their sensuality, and because of them the way of truth will be blasphemed. And in their greed they will exploit you with false words. Their condemnation from long ago is not idle, and their destruction is not asleep (2 Peter 3:1-3).

Peter warned the church that in the same way that false prophets arose among God's people in the past, the future will also hold false teachers who seduce people away from Jesus as Lord and Master. They may not overtly tempt the people to follow a different god. They may not try to get people to bow down and worship Baal, but subtly and surely, they will seduce people into disobeying Christ and denying Jesus in their actions.

Peter warned about "destructive heresies." This is more than erroneous teaching. This is teaching that cuts across the core of the gospel and the core of kingdom living. It's not only false or misleading teaching, but false practice. Peter does not say that only a few people will follow these false teachers, but that "many will follow their sensuality." He characterizes these teachers as people who give permission to "sensuality" or pleasure and greed.

They are motivated by money and pleasure. They will exploit God's people. They will deceive them for money, for sex, and for fame. Peter promises that these things will happen. It is not an optimistic prognosis. This virus will infect the church.

Peter's consolation comes from the truth that God will surely and swiftly execute justice and condemn these false teachers. He compares them to sinning angels who experience binding in hell until judgment day and to Sodom and Gomorrah, which were turned to ash. But God rescued Lot. In the same way, God will rescue the righteous who are "greatly distressed by the sensual conduct of the wicked." (2 Peter 2:4-10).

Does the sensual conduct of the wicked greatly distress you? Or does it fascinate you? God stands ready to rescue you from every snare of the devil. Follow him out of these unsafe places.

> They count it pleasure to revel in the daytime. They are blots and blemishes, reveling in their deceptions, while they feast with you. They have eyes full of adultery, insatiable for sin. They entice unsteady souls. They have hearts trained in greed. Accursed children! Forsaking the right way, they have gone astray. They have followed the way of Balaam, the son of Beor, who loved gain from wrongdoing, but was rebuked for his own transgression; a speechless donkey spoke with human voice and restrained the prophet's madness (2 Peter 3:13-16).

Peter went on to characterize these false teachers as those who are not worried about the judgment but revel in the fact that they can "get away with it" now. These people are characterized by lust. They long for other people's spouses. They are trained in greed and are experts in getting money from the people of God.

Peter says that they have "followed the way of Balaam, the son of Beor who loved gain from wrongdoing." Like Balaam, these teachers have an experience with the truth. They are in the church. They have had real experiences with God.

Peter reminded his readers of Balaam's incredible folly "but [he] was rebuked for his own transgression; a speechless donkey spoke with a human voice and restrained the prophet's madness." Balaam was on his way to curse Israel, but his donkey alerted him that he was riding into death and judgment. The donkey's cry spared him from judgment and allowed God to use him to bless Israel and prophesy accurately. If only the donkey's cry or the angelic encounter had changed his heart. It did not.

Balaam was only restrained by the donkey for a brief time. In the end, he went back to his original motivation with an unchanged heart. Peter goes on to characterize this journey:

> These are waterless springs and mists driven by a storm. For them the gloom of utter darkness has been reserved. For, speaking loud boasts of folly, they entice by sensual passions of the flesh those who are barely escaping from those who live in error. They promise them freedom, but they themselves are slaves of corruption. For whatever overcomes a person, to that he is enslaved (2 Peter 3:17-19).

False believers and false teachers are like clouds. They are driven by the wind. They have no foundation, no anchor, no way to resist the desires of the flesh. They keep being drawn by every temptation. And they draw others into temptation themselves. They are weak, and they weaken others.

They promise freedom from legalism, freedom from "religion," freedom from judgment. But they are slaves to sin. The freedom they offer is a freedom from the yoke of Jesus and bondage to the yoke of sin and the devil. They feed the flesh and starve the spirit. They give temporary pleasure in exchange for eternal judgment.

Contrary to the message of the false teachers of Peter's time and the message of false teachers today, repentance does matter. Freedom from sin does matter. Whatever sin overcomes you is your master.

> For if, after they have escaped the defilements of the world through the knowledge of our Lord and Savior Jesus Christ, they are again entangled in them and overcome, the last state has become worse for them than the first. For it would have been better for them never to have known the way of righteousness than after knowing it to turn back from the holy commandment delivered to them. What the true proverb says has happened to them: "The dog returns to its own vomit, and the sow, after washing herself, returns to wallow in the mire" (2 Peter 3:20-22).

Like Balaam, who had a true encounter with Yahweh, these people find themselves intentionally sinning against God even after they met Him in Jesus Christ. They taste forgiveness. They experience grace, but they turn back to their sin. Their lust leads them astray again. Like Balaam, their encounters with God are not enough to truly change their hearts. Instead they desire evil. They seek a way to fulfill their lust and their greed. And Satan gives them an opportunity to do so.

Peter compares this to a dog who throws up, but then later goes back to eat its own vomit or a pig who is washed clean but craves the mud and longs to go back to it. Balaam was given an opportunity to be a servant of God. He stepped into a true prophetic role. But he longed for the mud. He went back to the vomit. He sought money. His greed poisoned his heart. He decided to serve a god who would make him rich rather than a God who would make him holy.

Jude warns the church of these same kinds of people. His writing is stunningly similar to Peter's, noting that these people will sneak into the church and be considered part of the kingdom, with the intention of turning grace into sensuality. These people see all the mercy and love that God has poured out, recognize that the cross means that those who believe will never have to pay for their sins, and find freedom to sin and disobey God.

> Beloved, although I was very eager to write to you about our common salvation, I found it necessary to write appealing to you to contend for the faith that was once for all delivered to the saints. For certain people have crept in unnoticed who long ago were designated for this condemnation, ungodly people, who pervert the grace of our God into sensuality and deny our only Master and Lord, Jesus Christ (Jude 3-4).

The key to identify these teachers is that they teach people to deny our "only" Master and Lord, Jesus Christ. They teach people to disobey Jesus, to deny Him in their actions, to worship other gods. Jude continued to describe these false teachers and lament their behavior and the judgment that will come upon them.

> Woe to them! For they walked in the way of Cain and abandoned themselves for the sake of gain to Balaam's error and perished in Korah's rebellion. These are hidden reefs at your love feasts, as they feast with you without fear, shepherds feeding themselves; waterless clouds, swept along by winds; fruitless trees in late autumn, twice dead, uprooted; wild waves of the sea, casting up the foam of their own shame; wandering stars, for whom the gloom of utter darkness has been reserved forever (Jude 11-13).

These teachers walked in the way of Cain. They were jealous, and they judged God as unjust. They became murderers in their heart. They traded their ministry and their chance at salvation for money. Just like Balaam.

They fell into Balaam's error. They had an experience with God. They understood grace. They saw some part of God's character. And they turned away for present pleasure and present riches.

They perished in Korah's rebellion. They saw the authority of God, the majesty of the Lord, the supremacy of Christ. And they rebelled. They thought they could lead their own lives. They thought they did not have to obey the servant of God—Jesus Christ.

Jesus Confronts Balaam's Teaching

In Jesus's final words to the churches in Revelation He summarizes the story of Balaam and commands the church to turn away from teachers that follow Balaam's way.

> And to the angel of the church in Pergamum write: 'The words of him who has the sharp two-edged sword.
>
> "'I know where you dwell, where Satan's throne is. Yet you hold fast my name, and you did not deny my faith even in the days of Antipas my faithful witness, who was killed among you, where Satan dwells (Revelation 2:13-14).

Jesus's message begins with encouragement. This church had been persecuted. In fact, they lived in the center of Satan's activity and influence. They held on to their witness of Christ even during this persecution. They weren't afraid to speak the name of Jesus. They weren't afraid to claim His rule in their lives. They held on to their testimony. Even when they were being martyred.

Jesus mentions the name of Antipas—a specific martyr. We don't know Antipas's story, but his name and life have been immortalized in the words of Scripture. Some day we may have a chance to meet Antipas and share in the glory that Christ received when Antipas gave his life to hold fast to the name of Jesus and the Kingdom of God.

This was an incredible church. They were heroes of the faith. They were trading their lives for the gospel. How could we possibly find fault with them? Jesus saw them with love and grace, but He was not blind to their hearts. He was not blind to all that went on in the church.

It's a popular belief in certain circles that Jesus doesn't see the sins of believers, that we have all been forgiven in advance, and that Jesus only interacts with us as if we are perfect. But Jesus's final words to the Church in the Book of Revelation strongly correct this misconception. Jesus sees error in the church. Jesus sees sins practiced in certain congregations. And He sees the present sins in our lives. He lovingly and firmly corrects them, so that we can be free in our relationship with Him and safe in His leadership.

Jesus's prophetic messages to the churches in Revelation are powerful examples of how Jesus loves and communicates with His churches. He was honest with the church in Pergamum. He did not let them continue in error or dangerous practice. He corrected them because they were in danger.

> But I have a few things against you: you have some there who hold the teaching of Balaam, who taught Balak to put a stumbling block before the sons of Israel, so that they might eat food sacrificed to idols and practice sexual immorality (Revelation 2:14).

Jesus summarized the story of Balaam, reminding the church that Balaam taught Balak to tempt the Israelites with sexual immorality and idolatry. He told the church at Pergumam that they had people in their congregation who were doing the same thing. These people were tempting the saints with idols and immorality. This was not a single false teacher like Balaam. This was an entire group of people called the Nicolaitans.

> So also you have some who hold the teaching of the Nicolaitans. Therefore repent. If not, I will come to you soon and war against them with the sword of my mouth. He who has an ear, let him hear what the Spirit says to the churches. To the one who conquers I will give some of the hidden manna, and I will give him a white stone, with a new name written on the stone that no one knows except the one who receives it' (Revelation 2:15-17).

Scholars can only guess at what the Nicolaitans taught, but it is evident that they led the church into sin. And the church in Pergamum was responsible for removing them from the church. The church tolerated them. They made peace with their doctrine and overlooked their sin and the fruit of their teaching.

Perhaps they reasoned that these Nicolaitans, like Balaam, had a genuinely gifted ministry. Perhaps they felt that it would be too divisive to label these people false teachers. Perhaps they were deceived themselves and falling into error.

Although this church had stood strong for Jesus amid Satanic influence and had a martyr's heart, Jesus promised to wage war against them if they did not repent. If the church in Pergamum did not turn away from the Nicolaitans teaching and stop putting up with it, Jesus would resist them. They would not only be fighting Satan, they would be fighting with Jesus.

The same is true for our churches today. How will we deal with the Balaams we encounter? Will we tolerate their greed? Will we be deceived by their teaching? Will we justify their existence because of their gifted supernatural ministry?

Will we find ourselves seduced by the greed and lust they introduce? Will we become Balaam's ourselves and trade our ministry for selfish gain?

Jesus stands ready to war against the wicked, but he knocks on the door of every drifting heart with an invitation to come and dine with Him. Jesus is ready to meet with us. He is ready to fellowship with us. He is ready to let you taste His goodness and His love—His power and His mercy. Meeting with Jesus as He truly is, receiving His love and His word and letting it grow in the soil of our hearts is the way to life.

Balaam's way offers money and pleasure now. But Jesus offers each of us a seat with Him as overcomers. Though there is suffering for a moment, there are pleasures in His presence forever and ever.

1. Eusebius, The History of the Church from Christ to Constantine (Minneapolis, Minn.: Augsburg Publishing House, 1975), II.1.12.

EPILOGUE: THE TRUE PROPHET OF GOD

Balaam's way has always been popular. The prophetic has always had its diviners and its manipulators, the greedy and the false. God has always had His true servants and has always spoken to His people to call them away from idols and towards right relationship with Him. He reaches out to His children; He reaches out to those sitting in darkness, and He even reaches out to the false ministers who have gone astray, lamenting the damage done to His people and restoring the vision and definition of a true prophet of God.

Concerning the prophets:

My heart is broken within me;
all my bones shake;
I am like a drunken man,

> like a man overcome by wine,
> because of the Lord
> and because of his holy words (Jeremiah 23:9).

Jeremiah the prophet mourned the state of the prophets in Israel in his day; He was consumed by emotion. This was not only his own emotional response, but God's. Jeremiah had fellowship with God's feelings and his heart responded to the words that God gave Him to speak.

Receiving God's word was not an intellectual exercise to Jeremiah. It was profoundly moving.

In the following verses (10-15) Jeremiah explained that the land was full of adulterers and that this resulted in God's judgment on the land. He lamented that the prophets and the priests oppressed others with the social and political power that Israel gave them. They lived evil lives, not only in private, but practiced evil boldly in God's temple. God promised that "their way" would lead them into darkness and destruction.

God compared the prophets of Samaria to the prophets of Jerusalem. The prophets of Samaria prophesied in the name of Baal, a false god. But the prophets of Jerusalem committed adultery and practiced lying as a lifestyle. They encouraged sin in the lives of others. These prophets from Jerusalem spread sin through God's people and multiplied evil throughout Israel.

> Thus says the Lord of hosts: "Do not listen to the words of the prophets who prophesy to you, filling you with vain hopes. They speak visions of their own minds, not from the mouth of the Lord. They say continually to those who despise the word of the Lord, 'It shall be well with you'; and to everyone who stubbornly follows his own heart, they say, 'No disaster shall come upon you.'" (Jeremiah 23:16-17).

God used Jeremiah to tell the people not to listen to these false prophets. It is clear from these verses that these prophets were prophesying positive messages. They filled people with hope—vain hope, positive expectation that was in error. The prophets gave blessings to people who despised God's Word and to those who lived for themselves and did not follow God. They assured everyone that there would be no judgment or punishment for sin. They made everyone feel safe, secure and happy. But they were wrong.

> For who among them has stood in the council of
>   the Lord
> to see and to hear his word,
> or who has paid attention to his word and listened?
>   (Jeremiah 23:18).

Here Yahweh gives the test and definition of a true prophet. These false prophets did not stand in his council, "meaning the heavenly inner circle where decisions are made and oracles released [...] the place where the Lord's word is heard and seen.[1]" True prophets and a true prophetic people meet with God and God shares His thoughts and His heart with them. God gives them the mind of Christ, they receive Christ's thoughts, and they respond to them. They give God's Word, God's thoughts, and God's heart attention. And they obey.

If these prophets had stood in the council of the Lord and heard God accurately, they would have given the message of Jeremiah 23:19-20:

> Behold, the storm of the Lord!
> Wrath has gone forth,
> a whirling tempest;
> it will burst upon the head of the wicked.
> The anger of the Lord will not turn back
> until he has executed and accomplished
> the intents of his heart.
> In the latter days you will understand it clearly.

True prophets of God do not operate according their own will, their own choice, or their own plans. They must be sent by God, and they can only prophesy after God speaks to them. To run without being sent, or to prophesy without hearing from God is presumption.

> I did not send the prophets,
> yet they ran;
> I did not speak to them,

yet they prophesied (Jeremiah 23:21).

God, though grieved and angry with these false prophets, expresses regret at what could have been. These words of regret were mourning in Jeremiah's mouth, but they hold a great promise for those of us who seek to be faithful to God's Word. There is a way to be faithful. Things could have been different for these false prophets:

> But if they had stood in my council,
> then they would have proclaimed my words to my
> people,
> and they would have turned them from their evil way,
> and from the evil of their deeds (Jeremiah 23:22).

If we fellowship with God and experience Him, we can walk in a right relationship with Him. He will share His thoughts with us. We will stand in His council, and we will hear his voice. We will proclaim his Word, and people will turn away from evil and join in God's fellowship. They too can stand in His council, and together we can advance in faithfulness and love until we reach the worship before the Lamb on His throne.

Meet with Yahweh

Balaam sought the God of Israel for the wrong reasons and the wrong way. But he did seek Yahweh. We live in a time when

God has revealed Himself to all of us through Jesus Christ. Every single one of us has access to the throne of grace by the blood of Jesus, and He stands before us as our High Priest, our Prophet, and our King.

We have access to God and can hear His voice. We can meet with Jesus. We don't need rituals, sacrifices, or magic. We just need the faith to pray, listen, and read the Scriptures.

> Let us then with confidence draw near to the throne of grace, that we may receive mercy and find grace to help in time of need (Hebrews 4:16).

Submit to Christ's Rule

Balaam sought to rule his own life. He wanted to be in charge. He saw the gods as powers to be manipulated and used for his own advancement and his own pleasure.

God loves you. He is the almighty and is worthy of worship and praise. He cannot be manipulated. And only His plan, His purpose, and His pleasure will endure for eternity. You can take part in His love and glory through Jesus Christ.

The truth is that there are two kingdoms in this world—the kingdom of darkness and the Kingdom of God. We all know what the kingdom of darkness is like. We have all experienced darkness in our lives. We've experienced pain, sin, and death. The ruler of the kingdom of darkness is Satan.

You may want to rule your own life and think that you can escape the kingdom of darkness that way, but really you can only build your own small kingdom in the kingdom of darkness.

The Kingdom of God is different. It's filled with light, life, and love. It's filled with God's presence and His glory. The ruler of the Kingdom of God is Jesus Christ.

We are all born trying to rule our own lives in the kingdom of darkness. But we only live a short time on this earth, and whichever kingdom we've served, we enter forever. All you have to do to stay in the kingdom of darkness is to serve yourself. At the end of time, God is going to destroy the kingdom of darkness along with all sin, pain, and death.

The Good News is that Jesus Christ came to this earth. He lived a perfect life. He loved you so much that He died on the cross for the forgiveness of your sins, and He rose from the dead so that you could have a new life in the Kingdom of God with Jesus as your King.[2]

If you give your life to Jesus Christ as your King and Master and obey Him, you can hear God's voice and avoid Balaam's way and Balaam's end.

> He has delivered us from the domain of darkness and transferred us to the kingdom of his beloved Son, in whom we have redemption, the forgiveness of sins.

> He is the image of the invisible God, the firstborn of all creation. For by him all things were created, in heaven and on earth, visible and invisible, whether thrones or dominions or rulers or authorities—all things were created through him and for him (Colossians 1:13-16).

Commit to Say What He Says

Even though Balaam's heart was not submitted to God, he had a commitment to only prophesy what God told him to. And he kept that commitment in the face of enormous pressure. I believe that this commitment was part of what gave Balaam the reputation that he had.

If you want to be faithful in prophetic ministry, you will have to set aside your reputation, your opinions, and your desire to please others and make a firm commitment to only speak the truth that God has given you to say.

You will have to stake your life and your ministry on getting God's words right.

> For we are not, like so many, peddlers of God's word, but as men of sincerity, as commissioned by God, in the sight of God we speak in Christ (2 Corinthians 2:17).

Pay the Price to Hear and Obey

Though Balaam was a pagan diviner, he had a strong faith that he could meet with Yahweh, and he was motivated to pursue words from God. Even though Balaam sought God the wrong way and with the wrong intentions, God still met with him. How much more can we count on God if we pursue Him in faith and sincerity?

Balaam was willing to spend his resources on meeting Yahweh. He made sacrifices. Balaam was willing to spend his time on meeting Yahweh. He was committed to seeking God on long nights.

You are not a pagan diviner. You are much more assured to meet with God through Jesus Christ if you determine in your heart to spend your time, your energy, and your resources to meet with God.

> Therefore, brothers, since we have confidence to enter the holy places by the blood of Jesus, by the new and living way that he opened for us through the curtain, that is, through his flesh, and since we have a great priest over the house of God, let us draw near with a true heart in full assurance of faith, with our hearts sprinkled clean from an evil conscience and our bodies washed with pure water. Let us hold fast the confession of our hope without wavering, for he who promised is faithful (Hebrews 10:19-23).

JONATHAN AMMON

Flee Idolatry

Balaam ended in disaster because of the evil of his own heart. But Jesus had provided a way of escape from every temptation and a way of purification for our hearts through the Holy Spirit. Immerse yourself in Jesus and the Gospel, and you will live in freedom from the idols that doomed Balaam.

The Epistle of First John has a jarring ending. After describing the gospel and Christ as God, a terse Greek sentence follows. In context it's so jarring that scholars argue whether it was added later. They wonder if the verse is out of place. After all, shouldn't John end his book with a positive conclusion pulled from the arguments he had been building?

John's epistle is a clarion call to truth and holiness. He exhorts His readers to cling to the "true God," not the false Christs and their false messages. He reminds his readers that those who follow Christ do not make peace with a lifestyle of sin. The result of false teaching is always idolatrous beliefs—false doctrine and false worship—and sinful practice. John was actively spreading the antidote to false teaching through the church. He was actively combating idolatry. John's final exhortation is as plain and simple as he can make His message.

I want to close this book the same way that the Apostle John closed his. I hope his exhortation strikes your heart in the same way it strikes mine.

Little children, keep yourselves from idols. Amen (1 John 5:21).

---

1. Brown, PhD, Michael L.. Jeremiah, Lamentations (The Expositor's Bible Commentary) (Kindle Locations 10578-10579). Zondervan. Kindle Edition.
2. Much of this section draws from a simple Gospel presentation called the Two Kingdoms which we use in the church planting movement I participate in. Chuck Wood and Jim Mcknight developed the Two Kingdoms as a simple and clear call way to make Jesus Lord and Master.

APPENDIX: BALAAM'S FOURTH ORACLE: AN EXEGETICAL ANALYSIS OF NUMBERS 24:12-19

Introduction

As Christians we have the benefit of the full revelation of Christ and the Scriptures to illuminate the grace and promises of God. Peter reveals that the prophets were searching to understand the time and circumstances regarding the Savior and Messiah and the "glories" that would follow his arrival (1 Peter 1:10-12 ESV). As believers, we search with the Old Testament prophets. We don't grope forward but look backward at the Spirit-inspired texts of Scripture which testify of Christ's suffering, the inauguration of the New Covenant, and the things that are to come (John 16:13). In the same way that Christ instructed His disciples, interpreting to them all the things concerning Himself in the Scriptures, we look to the Spirit to instruct us in what the Scriptures teach us about

Christ. This search for Christ in the Old Testament is also a search for faithful interpretation and obedience to all of Scripture.

The story of Balaam in the book of Numbers and specifically Balaam's fourth oracle in Numbers 24:12-19 remains one of the most debated prophecies in the Pentateuch. Followers of Jesus search for Christ in the text but must approach it faithfully as a text far removed from our current context. The story of Balaam is full of alien concepts and practices. Its people and places are far removed from the 21st century imagination and familiarity by time and place. Yet for those who believe that all Scripture is God-breathed and useful for teaching, Balaam's fourth oracle remains relevant for guiding us into truth and faithfulness (2 Tim 3:16).

Objective

In this work, we will examine Balaam's fourth oracle in light of its literary and historical context in order to demonstrate that Balaam prophesied (i) regarding the future (ii) of a king who would rise out of Israel (iii) that this king would destroy the Moabites, dispossessing both the Moabites and Edomites (iv) that this oracle has a partial, historical fulfillment in David, and that (v) the most faithful interpretation of the text for evangelical believers is that Balaam's fourth oracle has its ultimate fulfillment in Christ's first and second advents.

APPENDIX: BALAAM'S FOURTH ORACLE: AN EXEGETICAL ANAL...

Literary Background

The Hebrew title of the Book of Numbers translates to *In the Wilderness*.[1] God made a promise to the unbelieving and rebellious Israelites, "...your dead bodies shall fall in this wilderness. And your children shall be shepherds in the wilderness forty years and shall suffer for your faithlessness, until the last of your dead bodies lies in the wilderness" (Numbers 14:32-33). The Book of Numbers describes this journey to the Promised Land, the loss of the Promised Land, and the forty years of life, death, and judgment in the wilderness.

Numbers can be divided into five sections. Three sections contain the stories of Israel's life and God's law-giving in the wilderness. Two sections tell of Israel's journeys between these times in the wilderness: Israel's journey from Sinai to Kadesh, where the Promised Land was lost, and the second journey from Kadesh to the Plains of Moab. On the Plains of Moab Israel's journey comes to a climax in an encounter with Balaam and concludes with the next generation waiting to enter the Promised Land under Joshua's leadership.

After God told Israel that their generation would not enter the Promised Land, they tried to enter the land anyway and suffered military defeat. But after that first foolhardy attempt to enter the Promised Land without God's blessing, Israel won every military battle. Israel destroyed the kings and armies of every land they entered, including some of the giants that had frightened them at the entrance to the Promised Land. The news of their escape from Egypt spread through the land, and their victories up and down the Jordan shook the country with fear.

The news of Israel's victories and the power of their God reached the Moabites. Their king, Balak of Moab, knew he would be defeated without the help of a higher power. So, he sought out the help of the greatest spiritual figure he knew: Balaam of Peor. Balak didn't come to Balaam because Balaam was a Hebrew prophet. He came to Balaam because Balaam was a spiritualist from within Balak's worldview and people group. He was a Mesopotamian Baru—a practitioner of divination and magic.[2]

Balak promised Balaam wealth and honor if he would curse Israel and weaken their forces. The story of Balaam can be divided into two sections: Balak's attempts to hire Balaam, and Balak's attempts to have Balaam curse Israel.[3] God resisted Balaam throughout the story, most notably in the interlude between the two sections, which feature the story of Balaam's talking donkey.

Numbers 24:12-19 occurs at the end of the second section of the Balaam story, and it stands as a climactic declaration of Israel's hope. God not only blessed Israel but promised overwhelming victory over her enemies in the future. Unfortunately, this story is followed by Israel's disobedience. Balaam counseled Israel's enemies to seduce Israel with idolatry and sexual immorality rather than fight them (Numbers 31:16).

APPENDIX: BALAAM'S FOURTH ORACLE: AN EXEGETICAL ANAL...

This counsel led to the incident at Baal Peor in Numbers 25:1-6 and God's judgment through execution and plague. Balaam's involvement in this incident becomes the identifying aspect of his life and character in the rest of Scripture.[4] Balaam's sin does not change the veracity or inspiration of his oracles, and though given to Israel's enemies in the Ancient Near East, Balaam's words in Numbers 24:15-19 still inspire believers today to put their hope in God and His Messiah.

Historical-Cultural Background

While the book of Numbers was written to God's people, Balaam's fourth oracle was not originally given to a Hebrew audience, nor did it come from a Hebrew or a follower of Yahweh. Balaam's fourth oracle was the result of the Spirit of God coming upon and empowering a Mesopotamian diviner to prophesy to a Moabite king about the destruction of his people and the future victory of God's people. This prophecy is removed from the 21st century western context by several layers. The historical actions occur between two Ancient Near Eastern polytheists outside of covenant with God. To make matters even more complex, Balak and Balaam seem to have different understandings of their interactions with the supernatural.

Balaam's words apply to people groups and geography of the Ancient Near East. The historical events surrounding his words and his prophecies were then related to the Ancient Near Eastern Israelites through the author of the book of

Numbers.[5] The original audience of the book of Numbers would have been far more familiar with Balak and Balaam's worldview, but the events occurred outside of even their culture. To understand the background of Numbers 24:12-19 we must do our best to understand Balak and Balaam's culture and worldview as well as the culture and worldview of the original author and audience of the book of Numbers.

Balak wasn't seeking general advice or help from Balaam. He had a specific plan in mind. He would pay Balaam to curse his enemies. Balak had a plan for how this should go. He would pay Balaam the appropriate price and provide the material for divination; in this case animals for sacrifice and perhaps liver reading. Balaam would then use these sacrifices to obtain power from the appropriate gods for an effective curse. In Balak's mind, he wasn't asking for someone to tell the future or divine the gods' will. He believed Balaam had the ability to manipulate the gods and use blessing and cursing power as he wished.[6]

Ancient Near Eastern people believed in the power of the spoken word, and Balak used a form of the Hebrew word for "curse" three times in verse six. Curses were viewed as pronouncements that bound magical forces and constrained the gods to bring about the consequences of the curse. They were viewed as automatically fulfilled unless another force opposed or annulled them.[7]

Balaam seems to have had a more complex view of spirituality than Balak. He truly believed that his power came from the

APPENDIX: BALAAM'S FOURTH ORACLE: AN EXEGETICAL ANAL...

deities he interacted with. He didn't see himself as possessing power to curse or bless on his own, instead he saw his power working according to the will of the appropriate god.[8]

Balaam seems to have seen his role primarily as an oracle, closer to a prophet than a sorcerer. He was more concerned with discerning the will of the gods and acting on their behalf. He had more respect for the gods and their abilities than Balak did, but as the story unfolds, it becomes clear that Balaam was used to having his way. In his experience, the gods could be manipulated.

The occasion of Balaam's fourth oracle is Balak sending Balaam away after Balaam blessed Israel instead of cursing them. Balaam comes under God's power and predicts what the people of Israel will do to the Moabites in the future.[9] This oracle was given to the King of Moab and the Moabites. Its original audience was Moabite, and it refers to geography and people groups familiar to the Moabites.

The historical events were retold for God's people, and Balaam's oracle to Balak, originally meant for the Moabites, was retold for the Israelites. Ronald Allen posits the audience of the book of Numbers as the generation of Israelites following the generation of Israelites who wandered in the wilderness and the three purposes for the writing of the book of Numbers as: "to compel obedience to Yahweh by members of the new community by reminding them of the wrath of God on their parents because of their breach of covenant, to encourage them to trust in the ongoing promises of their Lord

205

as they follow him into their heritage in Canaan, and to provoke them to the worship of God and to the enjoyment of their salvation."[10]

While first-century Western believers may be far from the Ancient Near Eastern context of the original audience, they are not so far from the purposes of the book. We can still be compelled to obey God through examples of his wrath on those who breach His covenant. We can still be encouraged to trust in God's promises as we journey toward His purpose in our lives, and we can still be provoked to worship God and enjoy our salvation.

The Primary Text

12 And Balaam said to Balak, "Did I not tell your messengers whom you sent to me, 13 'If Balak should give me his house full of silver and gold, I would not be able to go beyond the word of the Lord, to do either good or bad of my own will. What the Lord speaks, that will I speak'? 14 And now, behold, I am going to my people. Come, I will let you know what this people will do to your people in the latter days."
15 And he took up his discourse and said,
"The oracle of Balaam the son of Beor,
the oracle of the man whose eye is opened,
16 the oracle of him who hears the words of God,
and knows the knowledge of the Most High,
who sees the vision of the Almighty,

falling down with his eyes uncovered:
17 I see him, but not now;
I behold him, but not near:
a star shall come out of Jacob,
and a scepter shall rise out of Israel;
it shall crush the forehead of Moab
and break down all the sons of Sheth.
18 Edom shall be dispossessed;
Seir also, his enemies, shall be dispossessed.
Israel is doing valiantly.
19 And one from Jacob shall exercise dominion
and destroy the survivors of cities!" (Numbers 24:12-19).

Though Balaam's character remains hotly debated, verses 12 and 13 reveal that he had some integrity and the internal fortitude to resist Balak's insistence that Balaam curse Israel. Balak was furious and unconvinced either of Balaam's inspiration[11] or of his inability to compel the gods to curse Israel.[12] Balaam responded by saying that he "would not be able" to curse Israel regardless of reward or punishment. Timothy Ashley and others read this as Balaam arguing that he was morally incapable of going back on his word to both Balak and Yahweh that he would do what Yahweh instructed as well as physically incapable of transgressing Yahweh's command. Whether this was because he feared for his life or because Balaam felt he did not have the spiritually ability to accomplish the task is unclear.[13] It is possible that Balak and Balaam were speaking past each other, with Balak believing that Balaam could manipulate the gods to curse or bless as he pleased, and Balaam stating that he had no capabilities to curse or bless apart from Yahweh's will.[14]

Balaam's statement transitions into another prophetic oracle in verse 14. While the wording does not immediately indicate what spiritual experience Balaam was having, Gordon Wenham argues that Balaam's statement in verses 12 and 13 led to a trance with verse 14 as part of the revelatory oracle that Yahweh gives Balaam, and most scholars agree that God compelled Balaam to speak.[15] Balaam's words in verse 14 directly refer to the future.[16] While scholars are divided on whether Balaam's words in verse 14 directly refer to predictive prophecy or just advice, a number of evangelical scholars cite Albright's 1944 study which argues that the wording in verse 14 directly refers to a predictive oracle.[17] Regardless of how one takes the wording, it is hard to deny that Balaam was speaking of God's purposes in the future.[18]

In verses 15 and 16 Balaam established himself as God's visionary. Balaam did not prepare for this oracle with sacrifices. He did not search for omens or seek revelation of any kind. He spoke from a visionary experience as the Spirit of the Lord came upon him earlier in verse 2 of the same chapter. Balaam not only heard the words of "El" and sees the vision of Shaddai, but he also knows the knowledge of "Elyon," the Most High. Balaam's sensory experiences of seeing and hearing are complemented with an intimate knowledge that transcended human knowledge.[19] While the previous oracles revealed knowledge about the present and the future indirectly, this oracle explicitly revealed knowledge about the future, a knowledge that belongs to God alone and transcends human capability.[20] While Balaam's character may be debated, the nature of these words within the prophetic oracle are not. The narrator of Numbers clearly believed Balaam's words to be inspired prophecy, and Tobias Hagerland argued further that the Apostle John echoed Balaam's words in his own gospel to ascribe prophetic authority to Christ in John 3:32, 3:11. 5:30, 8:26, 38, 40, 47, 15:15.[21] Hagerland posits that John repeatedly alluded to the Septuagint's rendering of Balaam's story and oracles as a way to give authority to Christ's and the Apostles' prophetic ministry.[22] Balaam's words under the inspiration of the Holy Spirit are powerful prophetic credentials. Balaam was not speaking from his own mind. He spoke from intimate supernatural experience with Yahweh.

Verses 17 through 19 contain the predictive element of Balaam's fourth oracle. Balaam had a visionary experience in which he saw a person. The words "but not now" indicate that this figure is not present in Balaam's current context. "But not near," clarifies that this person that Balaam beheld in his visionary state resides in the future. These expressions combine with Balaam's words "in the latter days" in verse 14 to give a clear reference to the future.[23] The emphasis on future fulfillment and the term "latter days" does not guarantee far future fulfillment or eschatological fulfillment, but it is strong evidence that these prophecies are meant to refer to a

APPENDIX: BALAAM'S FOURTH ORACLE: AN EXEGETICAL ANAL...

fulfillment relatively later than the rest of Balaam's oracles and later than the near future with which Balak is concerned.[24]

But who is the "him," Balaam refers to? Balaam's opening is deliberately ambiguous, building tension. Two possibilities exist. The "him" could refer to God's people Israel, or to the "star" of the next line.[25] Whether "him" refers to the corporate body of God's people or an individual, the term must be representative of God's people according to verse 14—" what this people will do."[26]

The next lines refer to a "star" and "scepter." While it was uncommon for stars to represent kings among the Israelites, it was common among other cultures in the ancient near east.[27] This lends credibility to Balaam's oracles as coming from a non-Israelite source since astrological imagery would have been far more familiar and significant to both Balaam and Balak than the Israelite culture.[28] The "star" is paired with a "scepter," confirming the star's reference to royalty as scepter or staff clearly represents the position of a ruler and a symbol of authority and power.[29] Balaam's words may echo Jacob's blessing of Judah in Genesis 49:9-10 which states that the scepter would not depart from Judah.[30] The combination of star and scepter may combine the twelve tribes of Israel, the stars that Joseph saw in his dream in Genesis 37:9, with a single individual who represents all twelve tribes as a ruling king.[31]

The terms "star" and "scepter" by themselves do not demand messianic interpretation, but most certainly do refer to a coming king of Israel.[32] Whether or not these specific terms refer to a messianic fulfillment and to Christ is best examined after examining the rest of the oracle and interpreting the passage as a whole.

Verse 17 continues with the promise, "it shall crush the forehead of Moab and break down all the sons of Sheth." The coming representative king of Israel will conquer the neighboring nations, including Moab. The term "crush the forehead" or "skull" was a familiar symbol of defeating enemies in Egyptian, Ugaritic, and Hebrew literature.[33] The term is identical to Jeremiah 48:45, and Wenham argues that Jeremiah is quoting Balaam, more evidence of the inspiration of the oracle.[34] This part of the prophecy is clear: Israel and her King will conquer Balak's people, the Moabites. This is not a conditional prophecy warning the Moabites to not attack Israel.[35] It is an unconditional promise.

The next line is not as clear. "The sons of Sheth" could refer to three possibilities. Seth was the third son of Adam and Eve. If this does refer to Seth, as Wenham argues, then this verse refers to this King conquering or destroying a significant portion of the human race, potentially symbolizing all of God's enemies.[36] This interpretation would necessarily push the prophecy into both the messianic and eschatological realm. The phrase can also be interpreted as emphasizing the destruction of the Moabites from the line above, as the

Moabites were later identified with the lineage of Seth.[37] A third suggestion is that the phrase refers to a specific tribal people resident in the area.[38] Unquestionably this refers to God conquering Israel's local enemies in the future, and if this passage is messianic, it may refer to God's future enemies as a whole.

Edom shall be dispossessed;

Seir also, his enemies, shall be dispossessed.

Israel is doing valiantly.

And one from Jacob shall exercise dominion

and destroy the survivors of cities!" (Numbers 24:18-19).

Edom was Moab's neighbor and Balaam's view turns to the destruction of the Edomites who live on Mount Seir. Verse 18 parallels Edom with Seir in order to refer to the same people group who would be conquered and dispossessed of their land.[39] According to Deuteronomy 2 the Israelites were not to attack the Edomites because they were the descendants of Esau and God had given Seir to them. But Balaam saw a future fulfillment in which Israel does conquer and dispossess Edom, perhaps referring back to the curse that comes upon those who curse God's people (Genesis 12:3, Numbers 24:9).[40] This is further evidence of the far future fulfillment of these predictions.

Verse 19 emphasizes the reign of this king from Jacob who will not only exert his rule but destroy his enemies completely. Wenham argues that a rearrangement of the Hebrew provides better sense, rendering "survivors of cities" as "survivors of Ir." Balak had met Balaam at Ir-Moab or the City of Moab, and if Wenham is correct this means that Balaam shifts the focus of his oracle back to Balak's people and declares that Moab would be completely wiped out by Israel's conquering king.[41]

Theological Application

The Messianic Whole

For most Christians the star and scepter of verse 17 will immediately bring Christ to mind, who is referred to as "The bright morning star" in Revelation 22:16 and whose birth was announced in the heavens by a star in Matthew 2:1-10. These connections were seized by the early church fathers like Eusebius, Leo the Great, and Caesarius of Arles who argued that the Magi of Matthew 2 possessed copies of Balaam's oracle, which led them to follow the star that appeared at the Savior's birth.[42] These interpretations were subsequently denied by Martin Luther, who believed Balaam could not be worthy of such a prophecy, and these interpretations have further been denied or allegorized by a number of scholars and interpreters since.[43] However a number of messianic references to the star in Balaam's prophecy have been found in early Judaism, some even predicting that a star would rise in the east when the Messiah would be born.[44]

Later liberal scholars have argued that while Balaam's original prophecy did not originally suggest that the star would be messianic, it may have been later appropriated as a messianic prediction by Matthew's Gospel.[45] To an evangelical this would at the very least suggest that the Spirit spoke to Matthew, revealing Christ in Numbers 24:17 in a way that was not seen at the time. Liberal and evangelical scholars alike can agree that Matthew used a more charismatic first-century Jewish hermeneutic throughout his gospel that would have allowed him to use Balaam's text as evidence for Jesus as the Messiah.

The combination of evidence throughout 12-19 points to a future and messianic fulfillment. Scholars debate whether or not this oracle refers to David or Christ. David was indeed a king who rose out of Israel—a star and a scepter—and conquered both the Moabites and the Edomites three hundred years after this oracle, providing at least a partial fulfillment of Balaam's prophetic predictions. However, David did not destroy or dispossess the Moabites and Edomites completely. After the division of Israel into the northern and southern kingdoms Edom regained their independence and became Israel's enemy again and the subject of further judgment oracles.[46] If David was the only fulfillment of Balaam's oracle, then the evangelical reader must grapple with the prediction not coming to pass as explicitly written.

APPENDIX: BALAAM'S FOURTH ORACLE: AN EXEGETICAL ANAL...

Several possibilities exist. Either Balaam's words contained prophetic hyperbole, Israel's disobedience forfeited the fulfillment of this promise (unlikely as this prophecy was not given directly to Israel, but to Balak and Moab), Balaam erred, or this prophecy finds its ultimate fulfillment in Christ's first and second advents. Furthermore, if verse 19 does refer to Adam's son Seth, then the fulfillment must be eschatological as the oracle refers to the destruction of a significant portion of humanity.[47]

Additionally, the history of messianic interpretation in Jewish sources is difficult to ignore. Stefan Beverle, a scholar who denies the accuracy of Scripture's portrayal of Balaam, wrote a survey of the reception of Balaam's fourth oracle in its sociopolitical background. In spite of writing the survey to "stress the danger of (Christian) biases and pitfalls when 'messianic' texts are read historically," Beverle cannot help but conclude that Balaam's fourth oracle was referred to many times as a messianic prophecy during Jewish revolts in early Christian times.[48] A survey of the targumic versions of Balaam's fourth oracle reveals that most are both messianic and eschatological, openly identifying verse 17 with the Messiah and verse 19 with all of mankind rather than Israel's local enemies.[49] Allen similarly notes five citations as examples of Numbers 24:17 being regarded messianically by early Judaism.[50] While some scholars may deny that Balaam's fourth oracle refers to the Messiah, they cannot deny that both second temple Judaism and early Christianity saw it as a messianic prophecy.

Evangelicals have even stronger reason to believe this prophecy is messianic because of their commitment to the veracity of the text. David left the prophecy incompletely fulfilled, and those of us who believe in biblical prophecy look forward to the ultimate fulfillment of all of God's words and promises in the eschaton.

Conclusion

Balaam had a visionary experience from Yahweh in which he saw the latter days of what Israel would do to Balak's people, the Moabites. He saw a ruling king and deliverer rise out of Israel. This king would destroy the Moabites and conquer the land of Moab and Edom.

David rose as the king of Israel three hundred years later and conquered the Moabites and Edomites, taking their land. But Israel's dominion over Moab and Edom did not last. The Moabites and Edomites were not completely destroyed, and they rebelled against Israel and regained possession of their land, prompting promises of judgment from Yahweh.

Christ's first advent was announced with a star from heaven, and Christ truly is the King from King David's family who will rule on the throne of David forever. Christians look forward to the day when He will conquer all of God's enemies, defeat the last enemy—death, and usher in the New Heavens and New Earth, which He will possess perfectly forever. These truths are independent of Balaam's oracle, but

APPENDIX: BALAAM'S FOURTH ORACLE: AN EXEGETICAL ANAL...

those who believe them and believe in God's word through the Old Testament can look back and see Christ in Balaam's words.

The star that comes out of Jacob reminds us of the star that was shown in the heavens at the beginning of Matthew's Gospel and the bright morning star of Revelation who is Christ Jesus. The promise of God's ultimate victory over his enemies reminds us the promise of Christ's second coming. The words, "the latter days," "not yet," and "but not now" feel familiar to many of us as we anticipate the coming of Christ. Even in David's historical fulfillment of Balaam's words we can see a type of Christ defeating his enemies and ruling over His people. Scholarship debates the merits of seeing Christ in Balaam's fourth oracle; and perhaps only the disciples on the Emmaus road who heard Jesus interpret to them in all the Scriptures the things pertaining to Himself know for certain what God intended in Balaam's words.[51] But those of us who look to Jesus as our hope can find that hope in Balaam's words as we worship the King of all the earth who God brought into the world through Israel. We can trust that this King will return to conquer all of His enemies and look forward to the future glories of His conquering reign.[52]

---

1. Gordon J. Wenham, *Numbers* (TOTC; Downers Grove: InterVarsity Press, 2008), "Title and Contents."
2. Ronald B. Allen, *Numbers* (EBC; Grand Rapids: Zondervan, 2012), 22:8-11. See also "The sons of Israel also killed Balaam the son of Beor,

APPENDIX: BALAAM'S FOURTH ORACLE: AN EXEGETICAL ANAL...

the diviner, with the sword among the rest of their slain." (Joshua 13:22 NASB)

3. Michael L. Barre, "The Portrait of Balaam in Numbers 22-24," in *Journal of Bible and Theology* 51 (1997), 255.
4. Joshua 24:9-10, Deuteronomy 23:4-7, Nehemiah 13:2, 2 Peter 2:15-16, Jude 11, Revelation 2:14.
5. Traditionally assumed to be Moses based on the evidence within the Pentateuch and the assumption of the New Testament authors. For most evangelicals this evidence is enough to believe Moses was the author. See Wenham, *Numbers*, "Date and Authorship."
6. Allen, *Numbers*, "Notes 22:6."
7. *Ibid.*
8. *Ibid*, "Balaam's Seven Oracles (23:1-24:25), Overview."
9. Numbers 24:14
10. Allen, *Numbers*, "Historical Background and Purpose."
11. Wenham, *Numbers*, 24:9-13.
12. John H. Walton, Victor H. Matthews, and Mark W. Chavalas, *IVP Bible Background Commentary: The Old Testament.* (Downers Grove: Intervarsity, 2000), 160.
13. Timothy R. Ashely, *Numbers*, (NICOT; Grand Rapids: Eerdmans, 1990), 496.
14. Dennis R. Cole, *Numbers*, (NAC, Nashville: B&H, 2000), 22:5b-6.
15. Wenham, *Numbers*, 24:9-13.
16. Ashley, *Numbers*, 24:14-19.
17. W.F. Albright, "The Oracles of Balaam," *Journal of Biblical Literature* 63 (1944), 220.
18. Ashley, *Numbers*, 24:14-19.
19. Allen, *Numbers*, 22:15-16.
20. Wenham, *Numbers*, 24:14-16.
21. Tobias Hagerland, "The Power of Prophecy: A Septuagintal Echo in John 20:19-23," *Catholic Bible Quarterly* 71 (2009), 93.
22. *Ibid*, 102-103.
23. Ronald B. Allen, *The Theology of the Balaam Oracles: A Pagan Diviner and the Word of God* (Dallas: Dallas Theological Seminary, 1973), 312.
24. Allen, *Theology of the Balaam Oracles*, 313.
25. Ashley, *Numbers*, 24:14-19.
26. *Ibid.*

27. *Ibid.*
28. Wenham, *Numbers*, 24:17.
29. Cole, *Numbers*, 24:17b.
30. *Ibid.*
31. Roy Gane, *Leviticus - Numbers* (NIVAC, Nashville: Zondervan, 2004), Numbers 24 "Bridging Context."
32. Wenham, *Numbers*, 24:17.
33. Cole, *Numbers*, 24:17c-18a.
34. Wenham, *Numbers*, 24:17.
35. Gane, *Leviticus- Numbers*, Numbers 24 "Original Meaning."
36. Wenham, *Numbers* 24:17.
37. Cole, *Numbers*, 24:18b-19.
38. Albright, "The Oracles of Balaam," 220.
39. Wenham, *Numbers*, 24:18-19.
40. Gane, *Leviticus-Numbers*, Numbers 24 "Original Meaning."
41. Wenham, *Numbers*, 24:18-19.
42. Joseph T. Lienhard and Thomas C. Oden, *Exodus, Leviticus, Numbers, Deuteronomy*, Ancient Christian Commentary on Scripture (Downers Grove: Intervarsity Press, 2001) 24:15, 24:17.
43. Allen, *Theology of the Balaam Oracles*, 309-310.
44. *Ibid*, 310-311.
45. Tobias Nicklas, "Balaam and the Star of the Magi," in *The Prestige of the Pagan Prophet Balaam in Judaism, Early Christianity and Islam* (ed. George H. Van Kooten and Jacques van Ruiten; Boston: Brill, 2008), 238, 246.
46. Isaiah 63:1-6, 2 Kings 8:20-22
47. Wenham, *Numbers*, 24:17.
48. Stefan Beverle, "A Star Shall Come out of Jacob: A Critical Evaluation of the Balaam Oracle in the Context of Jewish Revolts in Roman Times," in *The Prestige of the Pagan Prophet Balaam in Judaism, Early Christianity and Islam* (ed. George H. Van Kooten and Jacques van Ruiten; Boston: Brill, 2008), 188.
49. Allen, *Theology of the Balaam Oracles*, 210-211.
50. *Ibid*, 311.
51. Luke 24:27
52. 2 Corinthians 1:20

SELECTED BIBLIOGRAPHY

Albright, W.F. "The Oracles of Balaam." *Journal of Biblical Literature* 63 (1944): 207-233.

Allen, Ronald B. *Numbers*. Expositor's Bible Commentary: Revised Edition. Nashville: Zondervan. 2012.

_____. *The Theology of the Balaam Oracles: A Pagan Diviner and the Word of God* (Unpublished doctoral dissertation). Dallas Theological Seminary, Dallas.

Ashley, Timothy R. *The Book of Numbers*. New International Commentary on the Old Testament. Grand Rapids, Eerdmans. 1993.

Barre, Michael L. "The Portrait of Balaam in Numbers 22-24." *Journal of Bible and Theology* 51 (1997): 254-266.

SELECTED BIBLIOGRAPHY

Beverle, Stefan. "A Star Shall Come out of Jacob: A Critical Evaluation of the Balaam Oracle in the Context of Jewish Revolts in Roman Times." Pages 163-188 in *The Prestige of the Pagan Prophet Balaam in Judaism, Early Christianity and Islam*. Edited by George H. Van Kooten and Jacques van Ruiten. Boston: Brill, 2008.

Cole, Dennis R. *Numbers: An Exegetical and Theological Exposition of Holy Scripture*: 3 (The New American Commentary). B&H Publishing Group. Kindle Edition.

Davies, T. Witton. *Magic, Divination and Demonology Among the Hebrews and Their Neighbors* (reprint of 1898 ed. New York: Ktav Publishing House, Inc., 1969).

Gane, Roy. *Leviticus & Numbers*. NIV Application Commentary. Nashville: Zondervan. 2004.

Guyot, Gilmore H. "The Prophecy of Balaam." *The Catholic Biblical Quarterly* 2 (1940): 330-340.

Hagerland, Tobias. "The Power of Prophecy: A Septuagintal Echo in John 20:19-23." *The Catholic Bible Quarterly* 71 (2009): 84-103.

Heschel, Abraham Joshua. *The Prophets*. Prince Press.

Houtman, Alberdina and Harry Sysling. "Balaam's Fourth Oracle (Numbers 24:15-19) According to Aramaic Targums." Pages 189-212 in *The Prestige of the Pagan Prophet Balaam in Judaism, Early Christianity and Islam*. Edited by George H. Van Kooten and Jacques van Ruiten. Boston: Brill, 2008.

SELECTED BIBLIOGRAPHY

Lienhard, Joseph T. and Thomas C. Oden. *Exodus, Leviticus, Numbers, Deuteronomy*. Ancient Christian Commentary on Scripture. Downers Grove: Intervarsity Press. 2001.

Nicklas, Tobias. "Balaam and the Star of the Magi." Pages 233-246 in *The Prestige of the Pagan Prophet Balaam in Judaism, Early Christianity and Islam*. Edited by George H. Van Kooten and Jacques van Ruiten. Boston: Brill, 2008.

Unger, Merrill F. *Biblical Demonology: A Study of the Spiritual Forces Behind the Present World Unrest* (Wheaton, Ill.: Scripture Press, 1952), p. 120.

Walton, John H., and Victor H. Matthews, Mark W. Chavalas. *IVP Bible Background Commentary: The Old Testament*. Downers Grove: Intervarsity Press, 2000.

Wenham, Gordon J. *Numbers* (Tyndale Old Testament Commentaries). InterVarsity Press. Kindle Edition.

Wenham, Gordon J. *Numbers*. Tyndale Old Testament Commentaries. Downers Grove: InterVarsity Press. 2008.

Zondervan. 2016. *NIV Cultural Backgrounds Study Bible: New International Version*. Zondervan.

FROM THE AUTHOR

I want to thank you so much for reading *Balaam's God* and spending time with Balaam's story. I would love to connect with. You can contact me at JonathanAndTatianaAmmon@gmail.com. I would love to know what you think about the book. You are the reason I am writing, and you are important to me. I also would really appreciate it if you left a review on Amazon or Goodreads.

ABOUT THE AUTHOR

Jonathan Ammon is also the author of *Prophetic Transformation,* *The Power of His Reign,* and a contributor to the *Paid in Full* and *Voice of God* training manuals. His writing focuses on holiness and faithfully hearing and proclaiming God's message. He lives in unusual places and likes to keep a low profile.

Made in the USA
Columbia, SC
10 May 2024

35511444R00148